D0119912

A 1950s
Childhood

A 1950s Childhood

From Tin Baths
to Bread and Dripping

PAUL FEENEY

In memory of my brother John (1946–2007)
and all the fun we had.

Cover illustrations: (front) a group of Glasgow children play in the
street (Mary Evans Picture Library); (back, upper) a group of children
enjoy a donkey ride at Weston-super-Mare, 1955 (author's collection);
(back, lower) a young boy playing in the street in central London
(author's collection)

This special edition published 2012
First published 2009
Reprinted 2009 (three times), 2010, 2011

The History Press
The Mill, Brimscombe Port
Stroud, Gloucestershire, GL5 2QG
www.thehistorypress.co.uk

© Paul Feeney, 2009, 2010, 2011, 2012

The right of Paul Feeney to be identified as the Author
of this work has been asserted in accordance with the
Copyrights, Designs and Patents Act 1988.

All rights reserved. No part of this book may be reprinted
or reproduced or utilised in any form or by any electronic,
mechanical or other means, now known or hereafter invented,
including photocopying and recording, or in any information
storage or retrieval system, without the permission in writing
from the Publishers.

British Library Cataloguing in Publication Data.
A catalogue record for this book is available from the British Library.

ISBN 978 0 7524 7941 5

Typesetting and origination by The History Press
Manufacturing managed by Jellyfish Print Solutions Ltd
Printed in India

Contents

ACKNOWLEDGEMENTS

I would like to thank the following people and organisations for giving permission to reproduce photographs in this book: Page 209 (bottom): Gwen Lippingwell and Denise Baldwin. Pages 10, 21, 66 and 209 (top): Remington Images. Page 200: Remington Images and Maria Cowdell. All other pictures and illustrations are from the author's collection. Every reasonable care has been taken to avoid any copyright infringements, but should any valid issue arise then I will look to correct it in subsequent editions.

One

A DECADE OF INNOCENCE

You lift one eyelid and poke your nose out from the blanket to exhale your warm breath into the freezing bedroom air, watching it condense into tiny droplets and form a fog that flows across the room like smoke from a cigarette. The hot water bottle lost its heat hours ago and has already been pushed to the very bottom of the bed. Your nose now feels `like ice and you dread the thought of sliding your leg out from the bedcovers onto the cold lino floor below. You struggle desperately to dislodge the sheets and blankets that your mum tucked in so tightly under the mattress when you went to bed last night, and at last you poke a toe out to test the cold bedroom air. Memories of cold draughty houses in wintertime with curtains hung behind the street door to reduce the flow of cold air. Woollen socks worn in bed, and thick, coarse, heavy overcoats used as top-up blankets to keep you warm. Frost that formed overnight on

Young girl dressed in a typical '50s outfit. Behind her is a baby in a pram and some young boys playing on the pavement of a street in central London in 1952.

the inside of bedroom windows, and the morning rush to get to the one heated room in the house, which was usually the kitchen or the living room.

No self-respecting child would ever rise from its bed without the repeated call from parents to 'get up', but this is Christmas morning and the extreme cold is somehow stifled by the anticipation of delving into the stocking that is hanging on the end of the bed. It is a sign of the times that the meagre contents generate such excitement, but this is Christmas 1950 and the expectations of an unspoilt child are modest. An orange, a two-ounce bar of chocolate and some nuts come as a welcomed treat in these times of post-war austerity. Getting out of bed on Christmas morning is less of an ordeal than usual because all of the excitement and joy of Christmas Day awaits! Has Father Christmas been? Did he eat the mince pie and drink the glass of sherry that mum left in the fireplace for him? Has he left me a present? These are all very important questions for a child of any generation to ask, but much more so for a 1950s child that is likely to have seen little in the way of personal treats in the months leading up to Christmas. Children waking up on Christmas morning in 1950s Britain had experienced government-imposed rationing of food and clothes all their lives. To them it was quite normal to go without the sweets, biscuits, crisps and fizzy drinks that would be taken for granted by future generations.

Everyone that grew up in the 1950s will have his or her own indelible memories of their childhood, but there were many common factors that would have touched and influenced every child from that seemingly gentle and innocent period. Cold rooms, tin baths, and outside toilets.

To a child, early day experiences are what life is expected to be, and the thought that things could get better is not even entertained. In towns and cities, the streets and local bomb ruin sites were often the only places for children to play and to expend their energy. It was a time when every street seemed to be full of children, with prams routinely parked outside houses to give the baby a good dose of fresh air. Residential streets were considered safe places for children to be left to play unaccompanied. Car ownership was still very low and most vehicles kept to the main roads. There was little need for motorists to use rat runs, and so side streets were generally traffic-free and without the danger or obstruction of parked cars. Most children were encouraged to be adventurous and they were expected to learn from their mistakes. Kids got dirty, fell out of trees, grazed their knees, and cut themselves. Most mothers kept a bottle of iodine in the house to disinfect the cuts and grazes of their wounded little soldiers. Head wounds might get some extra treatment, with a dose of smelling salts. Young boys commonly wore short trousers in the 1950s, and the telltale purple of the iodine was often to be seen on their knees. The sting from this chemical as it was applied was often worse than the pain of the accident itself. Once cleaned up and disinfected, the little soldier would be off to fight another battle. It was all part of growing up; there was very little mollycoddling of youngsters, it wasn't considered to be helpful in their development.

Kids were not analysed or studied for their greater wellbeing. There were no such things as health and safety or children's rights. Kids were taught discipline at home and at school, and corporal punishment was freely administered for bad behaviour. A child's role was quite simple: to eat, sleep, learn and play. When little Johnny got punished at school, he wouldn't dare go home and tell his parents because he was likely to get another wallop from them for having misbehaved at school in the first place.

The nation was recovering from the ravages of the Second World War and the camaraderie of wartime was still evident throughout the country. People had great pride in, and loyalty to, their country and seemed to share a common purpose in life. Everyone knew their neighbours and had a sense of belonging. There seemed to be a genuine air of humility among people and although many found it hard to make ends meet, there was a clear spirit of generosity. People were happy to surround themselves with modest personal belongings, and young couples were content to furnish their homes with post-war utility furniture. It was a time of innocence; children only knew the simple things of life and there were none of the peer pressures that exist today. People were grateful for the comfort of having shoes on their feet and food in their bellies. There was little evidence of jealousy or desire for luxuries. What you didn't have, you didn't miss! People were trusting and they frequently left their street door on the latch or the door key hanging down behind the letterbox for their kids to come and go as they pleased.

Children spent most of their lives outdoors, in all weathers. With children, time seems to pass slowly, and the long hot summer days of the '50s seemed to go on forever. Every day was an adventure, with a new street, bomb ruin, field or wood to explore. These were the playgrounds for the 1950s child. New games were made up all the time, using anything that came to hand. Bits of old wood, rope, chalk, sticks, rags, just about anything was adapted for playful use. You could play cowboys and indians or swashbuckling pirates using nothing but your imagination. Girls and boys played happily together but were divided when it came to some street games. Boys were expected to play rough and tumble games and to get their clothes dirty and shoes scuffed, but mums usually spent time grooming their daughters and they were expected to stay clean and be ladylike in their games. There was the occasional tomboy that would climb trees and fences with the boys, but generally girls stuck to their own preferred adventures and games. There was no set-rule that said boys shouldn't use a skipping rope, but somehow they were all useless at skipping! Why was it that girls could skip for ages without getting tangled up in the rope but they couldn't lasso a tree stump like a boy could? And why could a girl juggle two or three balls in the air or against a wall whilst singing a rhyme but couldn't kick a ball for toffee or even hit a ball with a bat? So many imponderables!

All girls loved to dress-up in their mother's clothes and proudly parade up and down the street in high-heeled shoes, routinely catching the bottom of mum's best dress in the heel as they obliviously went on their way. Their faces pasted with powder and lipstick, they did look a picture! True to their nature, boys would play war games and mimic the scene of soldiers returning from war by marching up and down singing 'We won the war in 1944' (and you thought they only did that at your school!)

Without the influence of television, there was no way for children in the early '50s to compare different lifestyles around the country. They knew that some people had more

Queen Street, Cardiff, in the 1950s. Note the old pram and 1950s trucks.

money than others and that some were very rich, like the Royal Family, who rode around in gold carriages wearing diamond tiaras, as they did when the royal procession went through the streets of London after the queen's coronation. Royalty would sometimes visit local areas and out would come the Town Hall's paintbrush. People joked that the royals must have thought that everything outside Buckingham Palace smelt of fresh paint! Some things haven't changed that much since the 1950s. Kids were aware that there was a social class system, and most knew at least one local child who was too good to play with the other kids. Rail travel was very popular in the 1940s and '50s, and trains were often used for family outings to the country or seaside. Railway stations were a good place to see a mix of social classes in one location, but the harsh separation of rich and poor people into first- and third-class train compartments soon made you realise what social class you were in. It was a very humbling experience to travel in the crowded third-class section with the 'riff-raff' while the well-to-do enjoyed the luxury of first class. The absence of second-class train compartments was always a bit of a mystery to young enquiring minds, but it seems that second class was abolished on most trains early in the twentieth century and thereafter those trains only had first- and third-class compartments, that is until 1956 when third was re-named second. The change of name didn't move you any higher up the social ladder but it made you feel that there was a bit less of a social gap.

Railway stations were cold, smelly and unwelcoming places, but there always seemed to be porters roaming around and it was possible to get help with lifting luggage on and off trains, particularly if you were travelling first class! The stations had big draughty waiting rooms with untended open fireplaces that usually only served to assist the cold draught on its way through the room. You would stare through the waiting-room window at the empty sweet dispensing machine on the platform and dream of the day when sweet rationing would finally end. Your dream was only broken by the choking smell of soot and smoke from the approaching steam locomotive. Some station platforms had a large machine where you could print your name onto a metal strip using an alphabet pointer and a handle to print each letter. The fascination of this machine was such that kids would even buy a one-penny platform ticket just so they could go onto the platform and try it out. Such simple pleasures!

Pathé news, at the cinema, was a great source of education about life in other parts of the world, as were the Hollywood films, which portrayed everyone in America as having loads of money, and of course illustrated how the Americans won the war for us! It's funny how children always enjoyed Pathé news and its wonderfully rousing theme music with the crowing cockerel. Cinemas would show two films, a feature and a B-movie, and between them they would show adverts and the Pathé newsreel with its dynamic voiceover narration. Cinema was always considered to be a proper night out and everyone would arrive early, often queuing outside for the one-and-nine-pennies, so that they would be sure to see the whole programme and not miss a minute – even standing for the National Anthem at the end. If you had the money then cinema was the best form of entertainment available to ordinary people. Whatever your way of life or dialect may have been, you were captivated by the wonderful magic of British and American films, and you will certainly remember those huge framed pictures of film stars that adorned the foyer walls and hung above the red-carpeted staircases in local cinemas everywhere.

There were, of course, big differences between urban and rural life, and in the early 1950s there was a noticeable disparity with food rationing when people in the countryside found it much easier to obtain eggs, butter and meat without rationing coupons. Most people supported the principles of rationing as a way of ensuring fair shares for all, but some people thought that the rationing system was very unfair on the poor and on the working classes living in towns and cities. Regardless of the government's best efforts to control the rationing of goods, there was a black market operating, and if you had money you could get anything.

Despite the hardships, there was a cosy feel to the 1950s. Mums usually stayed at home to look after the kids while dads went out to work, and they generally worked long hours. Some children had lost their dads in the war or had an invalid dad through war injuries. Mums were very important in the home, and as housewives they had a significant daily workload, but many also found part-time work to help pay the bills and to make ends meet. Mums went shopping for groceries every day. Perishable foods were bought in small amounts – just enough to last a day. It was quite usual to buy a single item of fruit rather than by the pound. Kids seemed to spend half their lives running errands for their mum or for a neighbour. You were made to eat all sorts of foods because they were 'good for you' – bread and dripping, black pudding, fried bread, fried eggs, mashed potatoes, sandwiches and chip butties. Everything that was put in front of you was said to be good for you, especially carrots – after all, you wouldn't be able to see in the dark if you didn't eat your carrots! Mums were forever baking cakes and there was always a child hanging around ready with a finger to scrape the remains from the mixing bowl and devour the remnants of the heavenly mix. We ate a lot of bread, eggs, potatoes or chips, and drank a lot of tea and milk. In 1950, bread and milk were the main components of a child's diet and 55 per cent of young children were drinking tea with their meals (source: Public Health Nutrition reports, National Survey of Health and Development, 1950). All mums could sew and knit. Mums were always altering clothes for growing youngsters: hems, sleeves, waistband and buttons were all moved several times before a garment was finally retired.

Mums would often dress siblings the same. This was more noticeable on girls than boys because the uniform colour, pattern and style of girls' outfits would be seen to be the same, whereas most boys wore a boring and inconspicuous white or grey shirt, grey flannel short trousers, striped elasticated belt with a snake clip, long grey socks and black shoes or plimsolls. All boys experienced sore chapped legs in winter, made worse by the rubbing from the seams of short trousers against their bare legs. The clothes on younger siblings were usually hand-me-downs and always looked too big, whereas the older siblings either looked too clean-cut in their new oversized outfit or pitiful in their old, now too small, garments. There was nothing worse than having to wear clothes that were two sizes too big, either because they were hand-me-downs or because they were bought to last you until you grew another two inches. Young girls liked to dress in pretty clothes but there was no pressure or desire for pre-teen kids to be fashionable. For boys, brand new clothes were always an embarrassment, as was a new haircut – a sure signal for mickey-taking! Clothes were just things you wore to make you presentable and to keep you warm. Apart from the blazer, working-class kids usually wore the same clothes in and out of school. Cleanliness was a byword for most mums. They made great efforts to ensure that their little darlings were well scrubbed and clean-clothed before leaving the house. This was followed by a compulsory check that each child had a handkerchief in their pocket, and then a lecture on how to behave when out and about. All mothers dreaded the thought of their child out in the street with socks down to their ankles and a runny nose, and the awful thought that they might even use their sleeve to wipe it. The shame of it!

Hair was a definite bone of contention for everyone. Girls didn't go to the hairdresser's but they were still much better groomed than boys because their mums would spend hours washing and styling their hair with curls, plaits, ringlets and ponytails. Ribbons were very popular and girls' hair was often tied with two ribbons on top. There were no hairdryers and so girls' hair was usually dried in front of the fire. They complained and screeched with pain continually as their hair was combed and brushed to get all the knots and tangles out. Boys were easier to deal with; short back and sides was the order of the day and if your hair touched your ears or your collar then it was too long. The unlucky ones had to endure the ridicule of their mates when confronted with the pudding-basin haircut that had been inflicted upon them by their dad. The lucky ones would be sent or dragged to the barbershop for a good all around shearing. The barber would put a board across the chair for you to climb up onto so that he could cut your hair at eye level, but what was in that silver can with the black rubber pump that he would use to dampen your hair down at the end? The barbershop walls were covered in pictures of film star hairstyles with all sorts of quiffs and waves, but when it came to your turn there was never any discussion about style; it was always the same old short back and sides. And

Young boy playing on his bike in the middle of a central London street, while behind him some girls are playing with their dolls' pram. The only sign of any traffic is a bus passing at the end of the road.

what was that 'something for the weekend, sir?' that men always sniggered about?

Some well-off parents did like to show off their little darlings on Sundays and at Christmas by dressing them in adult fashions. It was all right for girls but there was nothing worse than the sight of an eight-year-old boy kitted out in a miniature two-piece suit and bow tie. They would hang their heads in shame every time they had to endure this public humiliation.

Kids in the 1950s were no angels; they got up to mischief and there were some young scallywags around, but in the main they had respect for their elders. There was no mugging of old ladies and people felt safe to walk the streets. There was very little vandalism and no graffiti. Telephone boxes were fully glazed and each one contained a set of local telephone directories and a pay-box full of tuppences. If a public telephone was out of action then it was because of a technical fault and not because it had been smashed up by vandals. Many young boys carried a penknife but it was only used as a tool to whittle wood, not a weapon. When there were fights, kids would wrestle, punch, kick and scratch, but they would never think of using the penknife that might be in their pocket. Apart from the odd playground scrap involving hair pulling, girls were generally well behaved and didn't do much fighting.

All kinds of knives and weapons were openly sold in the high street shops and some wild teenagers did carry and use flick-knives and knuckle-dusters in punch-ups, but such fights were usually between gangs of youths and they didn't touch the lives of children. Teddy boys were tagged as being violent and could look threatening when they hung around in groups on street corners and in coffee bars, but many just wore Teddy boy style clothes for fashion purposes and were not at all violent. As with every generation of teenagers there was some fighting, but it was not exclusive to Teddy Boys; there were also Greasers, Beatniks and other non-descript young men that revelled in the occasional punch-up. However, any rebelliousness in unruly teenagers was generally knocked out of them when they got called up to do their National Service, which was still compulsory in 1950s Britain.

Young adults of the 1950s had lived through the terrible atrocities of war and experienced all of the post-war deprivation. This seemed to make them more protective of their own children and to value their innocence. Britain was nearly bankrupt and up to the hilt in debt to America. Nobody really knew what the future held for them and many people lived for today and were grateful for what they had. Children's ambitions were modest and most wanted to have a practical job when they grew up. Boys wanted to be firemen or bus drivers, and girls wanted to be nurses or air hostesses. Everyone hated wearing school uniforms but for some reason kids were attracted to jobs that involved wearing a uniform, probably because they had seen them glamorised in films.

Many who look back on their 1950s childhood will remember simple little things that have stuck with them all their lives: the taste of Farley's Rusk biscuits and thick syrupy welfare orange juice, toasting bread by the fireside, the rhythmic sound of your mum's knitting needles, Sunday afternoon tea at Granny's where the deafening silence was only broken by the sound of a ticking clock, *Mrs Dale's*

Diary on the radio, and the excitement of a visit to the local Woolworths store. 1950s weather will always evoke memories: the long, hot summer days playing outside were great but the cold, dark winters were horrible, and often boring because you spent so much of your time indoors. Those that lived in large urban areas, particularly London, will remember the dense fogs that would descend in the form of yellowish smog. These were often described as 'pea-soupers' because they were so thick. People would wear a damp handkerchief over their nose and mouth to protect them from breathing in the polluted air. The smog was caused by cold fog combining with coal-fire emissions from homes and industrial smokestacks. It was a very serious problem and thousands of people died from the resulting pollution. In 1952, extremely bad smog shrouded London and caused the premature death of an estimated 12,000 people over a three-month period.

The 1950s was probably the last decade in which children were able to retain their innocence through to the age of about twelve or thirteen. There was no peer pressure to grow up any quicker than nature intended. You were able to enjoy a carefree life that was full of childish fun and games, and the stresses of adolescence could wait!

Two

HOME LIFE

It's another cold and wet Sunday afternoon and you're stuck indoors with nothing to do. You kneel on a chair by the window, plant your elbows on the windowsill, and stare out into the street waiting for something to happen. The street is deserted. Everyone is stuck indoors, just like you! You detect a faint smell of roast beef coming from the kitchen, and in the background you can hear the dreaded sound of *The Billy Cotton Band Show* on the radio. 'Wakey! Wakey! Hey you down there –yes, you with the glasses!' You cover your ears to protect them from that dreadful signature tune *Somebody Stole My Gal*. *The Billy Cotton Band Show* has been on the radio for as long as you can remember, and it seems that you are condemned to a lifetime of Sunday lunchtime listening. There is some movement in the street, but no, it's only next door's cat scampering to get out of the rain. You hope that something will happen soon to relieve your boredom. Perhaps the rag-and-bone man will come down the road ringing his bell? Or what

This HMV auto-change portable record player with radio would have been a dream machine for any teenager to own in the 1950s.

about the knife-sharpener with a grinder on the front of his pushbike? Maybe the ice-cream man will come on his three-wheeled bike with the box at the front filled with small blocks of ice cream? No, he won't come; it's winter, and he never comes in the winter. By now, your knees are starting to get sore from kneeling on the chair, but at least the rain has stopped and there is a chink of light between the clouds. You shuffle about a bit to get more comfortable, and lean forward to take one last look down the street. At last! Something is happening! A Salvation Army band has stopped at the corner and they look as if they are going to pitch up and play (yes, the local Sally Army bands did go around the back streets on a Sunday). Hooray! The day is saved! The Salvation Army band drowns out the sound of the awful *Billy Cotton Band Show*. In celebration, you jump down from the chair and slide across the linoed floor in your stocking feet. Well worth the risk of a wallop and lecture about wearing holes in your socks.

Sunday was always a very quiet day and kids were often kept inside and told not to annoy the neighbours. Other than going to church or Sunday school and having the obligatory Sunday lunch, people just did relaxing things like reading the papers; then after lunch, snoozing in the armchair, pottering in the garden (in shirt and tie, of course) or going to the park. Apart from the corner shop that opened on Sunday mornings to sell newspapers, all of the shops were shut and the streets were generally quiet.

Even the mildest of winters were horrible because you spent so much time stuck indoors, and you longed for milder days to arrive so that you could get outside again. On cold, dark winter nights, there was nothing more warm and comforting than to curl up by the fireside and listen to a play on the radio. Only the occasional spark from the fire and the gentle clicking sound of your mum's knitting disturbed your concentration. Children were totally absorbed by the soft tones of the storyteller's voice purring from the speaker cloth at the front of a big old valve-radio. Even if the reader did all the voices, it was totally believable, and your imagination took you right into the scene of the story. Anyone that was around in the mid-fifties will remember the very scary BBC Light Programme's science fiction series, *Journey into Space*, which started on 21 September 1953. It frightened the life out of kids, but it was essential listening and had a huge audience – all those creepy sound effects and that mysterious haunting music. According to the BBC, by the time the series came to an end on 18 June 1958, there were 8 million people tuning in each week. There were loads of well-known people in it, including David Jacobs (he played many different parts), Deryck Guyler, Alfie Bass and David Kossoff.

Radio vs Television

When television sets first came into British homes they changed the traditional family lifestyle forever. The 1950s can easily be divided into two sections, the 'radio years' of the early '50s and the 'television years' of the late '50s. In the 'radio years', the focal point of any room was its source of warmth. Chairs would be gathered around the open fireplace in the living room, or near to the range in the kitchen. There was always a huge radio on a nearby sideboard. For some reason, you got more absorbed in a radio programme if you could see the radio from your chair. In the 'television years', all the chairs were arranged to face the television set, and you had to sit fairly close to it because the screens were quite small. In the 'radio years' children happily sat at the table and ate their tea at a leisurely pace, but television created an urgent need for kids to finish tea more quickly so that they could get to see *Children's Hour* on the television. No longer were children happy just to have the radio playing in the background while they ate their meals; television required their undivided attention. All those grey and grainy, yet mesmerising, children's programmes, like *Muffin the Mule*, presented by John Mills' sister, Annette; *Billy Bunter*, with Gerald Campion; *Crackerjack or* 'Crack-er-jack!', with Eamonn Andrews (Ronnie Corbett was a regular on the show in those days); *Blue Peter*, with Christopher Trace and Leila Williams (did you know she was winner of Miss Great Britain in 1957?); *The Adventures of Robin Hood*, with Richard Green and the lovely Bernadette O'Farrell, and in later episodes Patricia Driscoll (every schoolboy's dream), who took over as Maid Marian for the final two seasons.

In Britain, television had been around since long before the war, but even in the late 1950s, reception and picture quality was still quite poor. Whenever there was bad interference, the remedy was for someone to carry the aerial around the room until a reasonable picture appeared on the screen. There always seemed to be some image ghosting, but you learned to put up with that. Sometimes the picture would go completely haywire, and when that happened it was useful if you had a skilled engineer in the family to give the TV set a good whack on the top of its cabinet, which usually cured the problem. Whatever the downside, it didn't stop the growing demand for television sets throughout the 1950s. In 1947, there were only 15,000 British households with a television set. There were 3 million by 1954, and almost 13 million by 1964.

Around the House

The front room, or parlour, as it was often referred to in those days, was reserved for visitors and special occasions. It housed all the best furniture and many boasted a gramophone and an upright piano. These rooms were often just dust harbours and a complete waste of space because visitors usually sat in the kitchen or back room, which were more lived-in, warm and cosy. If you were lucky enough to have a kitchen larger than a galley, then you probably spent a great deal of time in there. The kitchen was the hub of the home, where all the cooking, eating, washing and ironing was done, and the baby was usually bathed in the sink or in a bowl on the kitchen table. Some kitchens even had a full-size bath in the corner that was covered with a board, but people living in older houses had to make do with a tin bath in front of the fire or a weekly visit to the public baths. The family pets were fed and watered in the kitchen, and that is where the dog would have its bed. Families often had hair-washing nights, when mum would mix a packet of Palmolive shampoo powder with water in an old jam jar or milk bottle; enough for the whole family to wash their hair – and in the kitchen, of course!

This smart 1950s HMV 2-band radio would have impressed the neighbours at the time.

Although magazines were full of pictures showing the latest fitted kitchens with all the appliances, in the real world kitchens were sparsely furnished with bare essentials, like cooker, sink, mangle, washboard, kitchen cabinet, and table and chairs. Stuff like Omo washing powder, Ajax powder and Robin starch were stored on a shelf under the sink, hidden behind a curtain. Fridges were expensive and still beyond the reach of ordinary families, but most houses had some form of pantry for storing food, with a wire mesh for ventilation. In warm weather, milk bottles were often stood in a bowl of cold water, and in colder weather, unopened milk bottles were kept on the outside windowsill with a stone on top of each bottle to stop the birds from pecking at the tin-foil top. The old 'whistle kettle' was a permanent fixture on top of the stove, and it got plenty of use in boiling endless supplies of hot water for tea and for washing. All mums seemed to have a sewing machine for mending and making things, and again the kitchen table was, more often than not, the place where such work was done. With so much time spent in the kitchen, it was normal to find a large valve radio sat on top of a kitchen cabinet or, if it was deep enough, on the mantle shelf above the fireplace. Many kids would do their homework at the kitchen table or, if that wasn't available, on their bed when the bedroom wasn't too cold.

Ticking clocks were a familiar sound around the house, but somehow you didn't notice them. There were various wind-up clocks in every room, even in the hallway. In the still of the night, the rhythmic ticking could be deafening, but nothing could keep a tired child awake.

Most adults seemed to smoke cigarettes and there were ashtrays in every room, even in the bedrooms. Peoples' clothes and all the soft furnishings must have reeked with the smell of cigarette and pipe smoke, but again, you didn't notice it. Air freshener products were not yet in common use and so rooms were usually given a good airing by opening all the windows to let fresh air blow through the house.

By the 1950s, many people were fortunate enough to have access to an inside toilet, but an awful lot of households still had to endure the hardship of using an outside toilet. Commonly referred to as lavatories, lavys or lavs, the outside toilet was usually situated in a small lean-to at the back of the house. These lavy lean-tos often had no light fittings and at night you would have to feel your way around and take advantage of any reflected light from the house. More often than not, they were cold, damp and draughty places that could be quite scary for kids. There were usually plenty of gaps around the door to allow the cold air to get in, and just to make sure, air holes were drilled near to the top of the door for ventilation. In wintertime, all of the water pipes and the overhead cistern had to be well lagged to prevent the water freezing. The sound of condensation dripping from an exposed piece of pipe just added to the overall eeriness of the place. To a child, the simple mechanics of using an outside loo could be quite daunting; the toilet itself seemed to be so big! Lifting the huge wooden lid with squeaky metal hinges was a task in itself for a four-foot-nothing wimp of a kid. This exposed the seat, or throne as it was sometimes called, which always seemed to be at waist height and required a great deal of stretching on tiptoes before you could get seated. Then you had to contend with the seat's enormous hole, over which you had to carefully perch with your hands pressed down firmly on each side of the wide wooden seat to support the weight of your body for fear that your little bum would fall through the hole and your whole body would be flushed away! Then it was time to make one of the biggest decisions facing a 1950s child; would you use the sheets of Izal toilet paper that were peeking from their cardboard box on the back of the lavy door, or instead opt for the neatly cut squares of newspaper that were dangling from a string on the wall. It was just another of those many childhood imponderables, why did we have to use these thin, shiny, slippery sheets

In the 1950s, a radiogram like this would be considered a real status symbol.

This popular style of television was described as a 'slim television' in the late 1950s, and was suitable for any size room.

of Izal toilet paper when newspaper was so much more absorbent and effective? Izal had the answer emblazoned on each sharply folded sheet, with the words 'medicated with Izal germicide'. Yes, it was more hygienic but you needed to use about a dozen sheets and it still didn't seem to do the job! However, Izal toilet paper was see-through and could act as a good alternative for tracing paper; children regularly used it as a substitute for the real thing. And by the way, what was that piece of flannel for that was always hanging on the back of the toilet door? There was usually no sink in the outside lavy but there always seemed to be a flannel or small towel hanging on the back of every lavy door. I dread to think!

Food and Drink

There had been vegetarians in Britain for over a hundred years, but they must have been very small in number back in the '50s, and it is unlikely there were any among post-war working-class families. The austere 1950s didn't really cater for people with dietry preferences. People generally ate what was available, and meat was considered to be a necessary source of protein and essential nutrients for healthy growing children and working adults. Kids were very active and used up lots of energy. They needed feeding and, in the main, they were given what was thought to be good for them rather than what they liked. It was considered important to have three square meals a day, and when money was scarce you would fill up on bread and potatoes.

What you had for breakfast was usually dependent upon what you could afford, and whether your mum worked and how much time she had to prepare it. During the week, most kids would have cereal, porridge, or a lightly boiled egg with bread soldiers to dip in. A full breakfast or 'fry-up' was usually reserved for the weekend when, if you could afford it, breakfast became a real meal, with bacon, egg, sausage, tomatoes, baked beans, and black pudding with fried bread. Everything except the baked beans was fried. There was always a fresh pot of tea being made. It was tea with everything; it was just second nature and coffee was too expensive to drink regularly throughout the day.

For main meals there were lots of stews and homemade meat pies, always with loads of potatoes and fresh 'in season' vegetables. You were always made to eat everything on your plate – 'eat your greens up or you won't grow'. Everyone that could afford it had a traditional roast dinner on Sunday, with roast beef, pork or lamb and roast potatoes, and loads of vegetables and gravy. Chicken was too expensive and usually reserved for Christmas. Sunday's leftovers were served up on Monday and Tuesday in the form of stew, meat pie, or cold meat dishes. During the rest of the week you would have a variety of wholesome dishes for dinner, including liver and bacon, bangers and mash, lamb or pork chops, egg and chips, toad-in-the-hole, bubble and squeak, and fish and chips on Fridays. There was always plenty of bread on the table to fill up on and a jug of water to wash it all down.

In summer, there were boring cold meat salads to contend with, only made tolerable by lashings of salad cream. So much adventure playtime was wasted while stuck indoors and pushing a piece of cucumber or cold lettuce around on your plate.

Puddings, sweets or 'afters', as they were often called, were usually a luxury reserved for Sundays. Rice pudding, bread and butter pudding, and semolina or tapioca milk puddings – you either loved them or hated them! Homemade spotted dick or apple pie served with Bird's yellow custard with the skin on top, or if you were really posh you might have pink blancmange. Pineapple chunks with Carnation milk, jelly and ice cream, trifle, and the occasional luxury of a block of Neapolitan ice cream.

A large slab of Lard cooking fat was ever present in the 1950s kitchen. It seemed to be a part of every mum's essential cooking ingredients. It went into everything – pies, cakes, bread, and biscuits – nothing was spared from a good chunk of Lard. It was even spread on bread as an alternative to butter, but it could never quite compare to the delicious taste of homemade beef or pork dripping, which was formed from the fat and liquid that was left in the pan after mum had cooked a joint of beef or pork. And who can forget the scrumptious taste of fish and chips cooked in beef dripping?

Welsh rarebit! Although often referred to as Welsh rarebit, in most households it was usually just a basic cheese on toast, made with plain cheddar cheese. No fancy Welsh rarebit recipes needed to entice a hungry child to eat it as a teatime or supper snack. On the other hand, there was nothing more likely to cause the sudden loss of appetite than the sight of a curled-up Spam sandwich being pushed in your direction across the table. Spam was a cheap substitute for ham but it was mystery meat; the colour, texture and taste didn't resemble real ham. It was a type of processed meat, made mostly from pork, but you were never quite sure what Spam was! Could there be a child of the '50s who actually liked the stuff?

Other popular sandwich fillings included such diverse things as mashed potatoes, chips, bananas, jam, salad cream, cheese, and of course fish paste, the ingredients of which was another childhood mystery!

Washdays

The growth in ownership of modern-day household appliances was seriously hindered by the economic impact of the Second World War on Britain's consumer market. As was the case with most labour-saving devices for the home, we were well behind the United States, where a large majority of homes already had an electric washing machine. In the late 1950s, less than a third of households in Britain had a washing machine, and these were single tub, top-loading machines, with a wringer on top. Most people were still washing by hand, using a scrubbing brush, washboard, and a hand-operated mangle. There were launderettes, but they were few and far between, and they were also expensive to use. In the cities and larger towns, there were laundry shops where people would take their dirty white cotton clothes, towels and bed sheets to be washed by machine. These places were called the 'bagwash', because you would put all your dirty stuff inside a heavy-duty cloth bag and then take the bag to the shop, where it would be weighed and tagged with a piece of cloth that was indelibly marked with your name or code number. The 'bagwash' was usually just an empty shop with a small counter, and a large set of scales that sat on the bare wooden floorboards. After your bag had been tagged, the lady behind the counter would heave it onto a stack of other bags that were piled high against the back wall of the shop, where they would all stay until the laundry van collected them later in the day. Some 'bagwash' shops only opened one day a week for dropping off washing, and another day for collecting it. These would be known as the 'bagwash' days for the local area. When your mum collected the bagwash it would smell of chemicals and still be damp, just right for mum's favourite job – ironing. You only took white cotton things to the 'bagwash' because everything was bleached and boiled in the laundry – bed mites didn't stand a chance!

Tradesmen and Services

It was a time when many people felt at ease to leave the street door on the latch, except at night or if the house was empty, and they would leave a key hanging down behind the letterbox just in case someone did get locked out. Apart from the noise of kids playing, the streets were usually fairly quiet places and so not much went unnoticed. There were the regular well-known deliverymen like the postman, milkman, breadman, coalman, and of course 'the man from the Pru'. Everyone seemed to have the Prudential Insurance man call each week to collect the small life insurance premiums. Before the age of telesales, when most people didn't even have a telephone, the door-to-door salesmen were very active. The tallyman would call door-to-door selling goods on the never-never. They were so convincing – 'you can have all this for just a shilling a week!' It really is true that some people would hide behind the sofa when he knocked on the door for his money. Many of the inner-city travelling salesmen would ride pushbikes, and some used the earliest mopeds, which were just basic pushbikes with a small motor attached to the top of the front tyre. There was a profusion of brush and cleaning equipment salesmen, and of course the ever popular and very convincing *Encyclopaedia Britannica* salesmen, offering the whole twenty-four-volume set of encyclopaedias on an easy payment plan. No child could hope to pass the eleven-plus exams without access to their very own set of encyclopaedias.

Postmen always looked smart with their top-to-toe uniform, which included a shirt and tie, a lapel badge carrying the postman's number, and a flat 'military style' peaked cap with a badge that featured a post horn and St Edward's crown. The post would drop through the letterbox at about 7am each day and there would be a second delivery later in the morning.

The telegram boy, in his navy blue uniform with red piping and pillbox cap, was never a welcome sight in the street. Few people had telephones and the fastest way to get a message to someone was by telegram, but they were expensive to send (about 6d for nine words and a penny for each additional word, including the address) and were only used to send urgent messages of joy, sorrow and success. Although they were traditionally sent to announce or

In 1953, this latest Esse cooker with boiler cost £91 4s 6d. Equivalent to about £1,900 at today's values based on the retail price index.

congratulate expected good news, like a marriage or the birth of a child, in everyday life they usually meant bad news, normally a death. The curtains would twitch whenever a telegram boy arrived in the street, and everyone's pulses would race like mad.

The milkman also wore a uniform, including a collar and tie and a peaked cap. The milk was delivered from either a horse-drawn milk cart or a hand-pulled milk float, also known as a pedestrian-controlled float. Each morning, the milk magically arrived on your doorstep before you had even poked your head out from the bedclothes.

Outlying areas would have groceries and bread delivered, and sometimes the milk would be delivered from an urn into your own jug and measured by the pint or half pint. Quite often these delivery rounds-men would become friends with their customers, downing many a cup of tea en route.

Coal was delivered regularly on horse-drawn drays or trucks. The coalmen were usually large intimidating men with faces and hands blackened by the coal dust. They often wore flat caps and sleeveless leather jackets. The coalmen would heave the huge hundredweight (cwt) sacks of coal off the flatbed dray and carry them on their backs to the coalbunkers, or tip them through a coalhole in the pavement into the cellar below.

Chimney sweeps were always a source of entertainment for kids. They would usually arrive on a pushbike carrying a few long-handled brushes and an old sheet. The sweep would have a permanent covering of soot all over, even when he had just arrived. All the furniture would be pushed back from the fireplace and covered with sheets before he arrived, but it was always a traumatic experience for house-proud mums. For the kids, it was amusing to watch mum's face and to hear her gasp as the sweep manoeuvred his brushes up the chimney and a cloud of soot bellowed out from beneath the protective sheet, dispensing a nice covering of black dust around the room. The sweep would always be carefully escorted from the house when he had finished to make sure he didn't rub up against anything he passed on the way. Then the clean-up would begin! In the 1950s, people were encouraged by the government to use smokeless fuel to help reduce the smog. Some people started to board up their fireplaces and fit new snazzy two-bar electric fires to replace the old coal fire. Some did it to be fashionable, but most did it to get rid of the mess and inconvenience of fetching the coal in from the cold cellar or outside bunker.

Window cleaners were plentiful, with their stepladder and bucket anchored onto their pushbike. Sometimes window cleaners would carry their stuff in a homemade wooden box (like a sidecar) attached to the side of their bike. Most people didn't have the money to pay for window cleaning and so they did it themselves. It wasn't beyond a window cleaner's cheek to knock and ask for a bucket of clean water, even if he hadn't cleaned your windows!

The gas and electric meter men would come regularly to empty the meter-boxes of cash. Most people paid for their gas and electric as they went, via 'shilling in the meter' boxes, which the meter men padlocked and sealed with wire and wax. The meters were set to overcharge and so you would usually get cash refunded when the meter was read. Fish and chips tonight!

Paperboys were a common sight in the early mornings. Paperboy jobs were highly valued as a source of extra pocket money, but the paper rounds were usually quite big and widespread because most people would buy their newspapers on the way to work. It was unusual to see a girl doing a paper round.

Food ration books issued by the Ministry of Food. Rationing of foodstuffs finally ended in July 1954.

Healthcare

Most homes had a few basic medical supplies on hand to treat the little warriors' cuts and grazes, fevers or infections. Aspirin, Beecham's Powders, Veno's cough mixture (at least a year old), a bottle of smelling salts, a tin of plasters, tincture of iodine antiseptic, and Germolene antiseptic cream with its distinctive hospital smell that reassured you of its remedial powers.

As a young child in the early 1950s, you ate quite healthily with high calcium and iron intakes through eating foods like bread and milk, red meat, greens and potatoes, and you drank very few sugary drinks. You were also very fit with all those exhausting and dangerous games you played, but you still couldn't escape the childhood illnesses. Chicken Pox, Measles, Whooping Cough, German Measles, Mumps and Tonsillitis; you got them all. In the early 1950s, before immunisation started in 1955, there was a great fear of catching polio. It was a horrible disease that crippled thousands of children and, sadly, killed many. It wasn't unusual to see children with crutches, leg callipers or corrective shoes after contracting polio. Diphtheria was a big killer prior to the introduction of nationwide immunisation in the 1940s, which resulted in a dramatic fall in the number of reported cases. In 1940, there were 3,283 deaths in the UK, compared with just six deaths from the disease in 1957. Tuberculosis (TB) was also a big concern in Britain up until the BCG vaccination was introduced in 1953; but even then TB didn't disappear entirely.

Winter always brought the misery of colds and flu, and minor infections like earache were common, as were involuntary nosebleeds and fight-inflicted bloody noses. The walking wounded were to be seen everywhere; a child with his or her arm or leg in plaster, a temporary eye patch, or a leather fingerstall tied around the wrist, were all familiar sights.

If you needed to see the doctor, it seemed easy. You didn't have to make an appointment; you just turned up at the surgery and waited your turn. Doctors' waiting rooms were small intimate places, simply furnished with rows of hardback wooden chairs. There was no receptionist to manage the patients and doctors would retrieve patients' notes from filing cabinets themselves. Apart from the wooden chairs, the only accessory in the waiting room was the bell or buzzer to summon the next patient into the surgery. Doctors did a lot of home visits; if your mum said you were ill in bed, the doctor came out without any fuss. It all seemed very efficient and free of paperwork. In the early 1950s, you definitely didn't want to hear the doctor say that you needed an injection. They were still using re-usable needles then, and they were so big! The doctor would ask your mum to boil the needle in a saucepan of water for a few minutes to sterilise it. That would add to the trauma, with so much more time for the patient to think about it. The injections made a huge hole in the fleshy part of your tiny arm or backside, and they really hurt.

If you were confined to bed with some dreaded lurgy, then you had to have a bottle of Lucozade and a bunch of grapes next to the bed, even if you didn't like grapes. The Lucozade was supposed to give you energy and most kids loved it. You had to drink it while you could because it was expensive and was only bought when someone was ill.

Although we had free healthcare under the newly created National Health Service (established 1948), from 1952 it cost your mum a shilling to get a doctor's prescription form filled in at the chemist, and this charge was increased to one shilling per item in 1956.

There was also a charge of £1 introduced for dental treatment in 1952. No child of the '50s will ever forget the dreaded visits to the dentist. It was the stuff of nightmares! That horrible cube of dry wadding that the dentist would shove under your back teeth to keep your mouth open, and the awful smell of the black rubber face-mask that was held over your nose and mouth to administer the anaesthetic gas that would send you to sleep and into a world of hallucinatory nightmarish dreams. Afterwards, you drifted back into consciousness tasting the disgusting mix of bleeding gums and residual gas in your mouth, and the nausea inevitably brought on bouts of uncontrollable vomiting. The horrendous experience didn't end at the dentist's door because the soreness, nausea and dizziness could last for several hours. Who could question why a child of the '50s would often need to be dragged screaming and shouting to the dentist's chair?

Any child that was hospitalised in the 1950s will remember the Nightingale wards, named after Florence Nightingale, with rows of beds each side of a long room and large tables in the middle where the nurses did their paperwork and held meetings. The nurses were always so clean and smart in their uniforms, with white starched bib-front pinafore dresses and caps, and blue elasticated belts with a crest on the buckle. Most had an upside-down watch pinned to the top of their pinafore for use when they checked patients' pulses. Was there ever a boy with a slow pulse reading? Most young girls wanted to be a nurse and the boys wanted to marry one! The smell of ether was ever present throughout hospital buildings, but if you were an inpatient you soon got used to it. For young kids, hospitals were lonely places and you could feel abandoned. You were often placed in adult wards and up until 1954, children in hospital were only allowed to see their parents on Saturdays and Sundays, and only for a short time. The hospitals were run very formally, with Matron's daily inspections sending every nurse into a panic, but you were very well looked after, and the doctors and nurses were wonderful.

Three

THE STREETS AND BOMB RUINS

There you are, out in the street wearing your new Davy Crockett fur hat and a belt with double holsters strapped to your legs, looking down the barrel of a Roy Rogers silver six-shooter cap-gun, and you have just run out of caps for your Wyatt Earp style long barrel shotgun. Nothing for it but to run home and get your spud-gun and one of mums big baking potatoes for ammunition.

'Come on, get out of that bed, it's eight o'clock and you can't lie there all day!' Blimey, you can't even get a lie-in on a Saturday morning! You turn over and curl up again for another minute's shut-eye while you try to pick up the threads of your broken dream. No, you haven't really got the latest six-shooter cap-gun with matching holsters, but you've seen one in your local Woolworths store and you dream of having it, along with all the other trappings of your big-screen cowboy heroes. You have got a Davy

Crockett fur hat that your mum made for you, but sadly, your cowboy adventures are usually played out with guns and rifles made from sticks and lumps of wood that you have whittled into shape with your penknife, and the sound effects are just primitive 'bang-bangs' that you shout as you aim your deadly weapon at the escaping bandits.

'Come on, get out of that bed, it's a quarter past eight and your mates will be knocking for you soon!' Yes, I must get up or I'll be late for Saturday Morning Pictures at the Odeon!

If you lived in, or near to, a town in the 1950s then the highlight of your week was Saturday Morning Pictures at the local cinema. Other than that, weather permitting, most of your spare time would have been spent outside enjoying the thrills and spills of childhood.

Many towns and cities across the country were badly damaged during the Second World War 'Blitz' bombing by Nazi Germany, with over a million houses destroyed or damaged in London alone. More than a decade later the evidence was still clear to see, with dilapidated houses and bomb ruins everywhere. These, together with derelict land created through the post-war slum clearance programmes, became the forbidden playgrounds of the post-war baby boomers. The local council housing estates and tenement buildings usually had their own concrete playgrounds or play areas, but these were characterless places, and local kids would usually venture out onto the streets to find adventure and mischief away from prying eyes. The local parks had children's play areas or 'swing gardens', as they were called. These always had a park keeper or warden dressed in full uniform with a peaked cap. The

A busy children's playground in Ayr in 1954, with lots of children playing on all sorts of equipment, including a roundabout, swings and slides.

park keepers, who often walked with a limp from an old war injury and were cruelly mimicked by the kids, would officiate in military style and it wouldn't be long before someone was being thrown out of the park for messing around on the equipment.

There were certain places that you would go to play depending on what you were planning to do. A derelict house used for a game of swashbuckling pirates would act as your ship, and the local woods might either be your jungle for playing Tarzan or your forest for playing Robin Hood.

Sometimes, you gave these places special code names; the alleyway for a game of Tin Tan Tommy would be called Tin Can Alley, a fenced-in bomb ruin used for a game of cowboys and Indians might be The Fort, and an old air-raid shelter used to plan the next adventure could be The Hideout. Many of the games and escapades were handed down from elder siblings, but time spent on the streets stimulated the imagination of younger siblings and they would often adapt an old idea to create a new game. Kids often had their own set of rules and values without really knowing it; word would get around about the places that were really dangerous to go to, or areas that you should only go to in a group. Gangs were just a group of kids that played together. There were no territorial divides and newcomers were always welcome to join in. Most kids were very streetwise and would steer clear of adults they didn't know. You knew all the comings and goings in the neighbourhood, and even how to avoid the local Bobbies on their beats. You were also very fit and could run away from trouble! Policemen were respected and feared; you might give them a bit of cheek from a safe distance but if you got caught then you would get a clip around the ear. You wouldn't dare tell your dad because he was likely to give you another wallop for having been up to mischief and for getting into trouble with the police.

Spring and summer were great because of the mild weather, long days and light evenings. A single day could encompass a great number of activities. Nothing was planned for; what you did was dependent upon who was around. If someone had a ball, it would only take seconds to start a game of football in the middle of the road, with jumpers for goalposts. A game could start with just two kids and end with fifteen. There were no rules; kids would just join in as they arrived in the street, but the game would always belong to the owner of the ball. If he got injured or threw a tantrum then it was likely that he would take his ball home and the game would end. Girls would often gather on the pavements to watch and shout encouragement, and the bravest of these would even attempt a kick or two of the ball.

Pushbikes were a luxury and so it was only the lucky few that had them. However, there was always the desire to have 'wheels' and much fun was had on home-made wooden go-karts, made out of old crates, lumps of wood and discarded pram wheels. You fixed an upright stick to the side, which you pulled back to scrape against the wheel and act as a brake, and there was a piece of rope tied to the front axle for steering. In winter, if you had snow, you would turn your hand to making wooden sledges and head for the nearest hill.

If you were bored, you could always go spotting car number plates on the main road, and wonder at some of the strange place names sign-written on the side of lorries. Then there were the train-spotting anoraks that would head off to the local railway station on a weekend with fish-paste sandwiches and a flask. But if that wasn't your idea of fun, as long as there was someone around for you to play with you rarely got bored. There were hundreds of different games you could play in any available location.

Pocket Money

You were fortunate if your mum and dad gave you your own pocket money to spend on whatever you wanted. Money was scarce and most kids got just enough to buy a few sweets and a comic. If you got a shilling a week then you were lucky; the *Beano* and *Dandy* cost tuppence each, and by the time you bought a few sweets you weren't left with much to do anything else. You didn't really need a lot because most of your free time was spent playing games or hanging-out with your mates, but sometimes, particularly during the holidays, you did need money for bus fares, or to get into the pictures or to go swimming. Fortunately, there was no peer pressure on kids to have the latest toy or to wear certain clothes, or anything like that. You could always bunk in to the pictures but usually you got caught and chucked out. Sometimes, one or two of you might get let in through one of the side exit doors by a mate on the inside who had already paid, but it was risky because you would all get chucked out if you were caught, so mostly you paid.

Enterprising kids found legitimate ways to earn extra money, but there was a lot of competition for anything money-earning. The newspaper rounds at the local newsagents were snapped up very quickly. Kids would team up to knock on doors and ask for any old newspapers, cardboard, rags and metal, and take them in an old pram or homemade cart to the scrap yard to be weighed and exchanged for cash. You could only do this every few weeks because it would take people time to acquire more of the same unwanted stuff in their houses. Neighbours never had a problem in getting something they had forgotten at the

This was the money we were using in the 1950s, long before Britain went decimal. The picture shows an old pound note, ten-shilling note, and all of the old coins, including a farthing, halfpenny, penny, three-penny piece, sixpence, shilling, two shilling or florin, and a half-crown.

shops, usually a packet of fags (cigarettes), because there was always an eager child ready to run errands for a couple of pennies. Collecting beer and lemonade bottles was a real money-spinner! When beer and fizzy drinks were sold, the price included a deposit of between one and three-pence on the bottle to get people to take the empties back for reprocessing, but many people discarded the bottles, much to the joy of little mercenaries. Quart bottles of beer were the most profitable: sometimes you could nip into the yard at the back of the pub, pick up a couple of empties and return them to a pub down the road that was owned by the same brewery. Kids learned from a young age that when adults drank alcohol, it not only loosened their tongues but it also made them more generous with their cash. On a Saturday or Sunday lunchtime, you could sit on the doorstep of the local pub with one or two of your mates, all looking dejected, and it wouldn't be long before one of the neighbours would emerge from the pub with lemonade and crisps for all. Remember those old Smith's potato crisp packets? You always had to rummage around to find the blue twist wrapper of salt at the bottom of the bag? There were no flavoured crisps back then; we had to wait until 1961 before we could experience the first taste of flavoured crisps, which was chicken. Then there were the long narrow 2d packets of KP nuts; pitiful when compared to the huge packs of peanuts sold in the shops today.

In the summer, lots of local corner pubs had their annual pub beanos, when regulars took a coach or charabanc daytrip to the nearest seaside resort. The coach would be stocked with crates of beer and everyone would be in a good mood. All the local kids would gather around for the traditional 'coin chucking', which involved the occupants of the coach throwing any loose change they had out of the coach windows as the coach pulled away. It was mostly 'coppers' that they threw but there was always some silver coins. As the coach moved off, there was a mad scramble in the road to collect as many coins as possible.

Kids did all sorts of unofficial work to get extra pocket money, like helping local shopkeepers and tradesmen; and of course the local milkman usually had a little helper. This was all slave labour, but kids had loads of energy and didn't understand the true value of the work they did. If you could earn sixpence down the market for moving a few boxes then that's what you did! In winter, kids even pooled their money to buy coal from the local coal merchant and then sold it door-to-door from an old pram or pushcart. Unfortunately, there was no money to be earned out of babysitting. With so many large families around, there wasn't much call for paid babysitters. There was always an elder sibling to look after the baby, or a neighbour would do it for nothing.

To manage your pocket money you first needed to learn the complicated calculations of pounds, shillings and pence. Most kids picked this up quickly from a very young age, and even had a reasonable understanding of the pre-1954 ration books. The coins and notes that we all used in the 1950s have been referred to as 'old money' since decimalisation took place in 1971. The 'old money' was written down using the LSD symbols £ s d, which were abbreviations for 'pounds, shillings and pence'. An example of how it was written would be £4 3s 6d (four pounds, three shillings, and six pence, or four pounds three-and-six). The '£' symbol was used for the pound and comes from the Latin word *librum* (a Roman unit of weight derived from the Latin word for 'scales'). The 's' symbol was used for the shilling and comes from the Latin word *solidus* (a Roman gold coin derived from the Latin word for 'whole'). The 'd' symbol was used for pence and comes from the Latin word *denarius* (a common Roman coin). There were some peculiarities about the way we used and spoke about money. Sometimes, expensive items would be sold in units of one guinea, which was equal to twenty-one shillings, but the coin itself no longer existed in the 1950s – in fact, the guinea coin had not been struck since 1799. Money was often referred to by slang names such as brass, dosh, dough, folding stuff, lolly, moola or readies. A group of farthings, halfpennies and pennies were called 'coppers', meaning a small amount of money as in 'just a few coppers'. Something costing one and a half pennies would be called 'threehaypence' or 'threehaypenny worth', as in 'three halfpennies'. It was quite normal for a shop to only use shillings and pence when pricing up low-value goods, so a pair of shoes might be advertised at 49/11d rather than £2 9s 11d. There was no two pence coin but the words 'tuppence' or 'tuppenny' were regularly used by everyone. Money would sometimes be used to describe people, as in the term 'not quite the full shilling'.

Here is a list of the main pre-decimalisation coins and notes, with the old English slang words sometimes used to refer to them:

Farthing (¼d) (4 farthings = 1 old penny).
Halfpenny (½d) Usually pronounced 'Hay-p-nee'.
Penny (1d) (12 pennies = 1 shilling).

Three pence (3d) Often pronounced 'thruppence' or a 'thruppeny-bit', and the old silver threepence was called a 'joey'.

Six pence (6d) Also known as a 'tanner' or a 'kick'.

Shilling (1/-) Also known as a 'bob' or a 'shilling-bit'. (20 shillings = 1 pound).

Two shillings (2/-) Also known as a 'florin' or a 'two-bob-bit'. (10 florins = 1 pound).

Half crown (2/6) Also known as 'half-a-dollar' or 'two-and-a-kick'. (1 half crown = 2 shillings and six old pence).

Crown (5/-) (rarely found in circulation) Sometimes called a 'dollar'. (1 crown = 5 shillings).

Ten-shilling note (10/-) Also known as a 'ten-bob-note', 'half-a-knicker' or 'half-a-bar'.

One pound note (£1) Also known as a 'quid', 'knicker', or a 'bar'.

Sweets and Treats

The magic of an old dusty sweetshop with a high wooden counter jam-packed with boxes of penny-chews and other sweet delights to tease the pennies out of your pocket. Sherbet dips, Wagon Wheels, blackjacks, fruit salads, liquorice sticks, gobstoppers, sherbet lemons, Rowntree's fruit gums and fruit pastilles, Spangles, chocolate coins in gold foil wrappers, sherbet flying saucers, Bubblegum, Fruitellas, Catherine Wheels, Love Hearts, Refreshers, Shrimps, Sherbet Fountains, Walnut Whips, Barrett's sweet cigarettes with football cards, and perhaps a Fry's Turkish Delight or a packet of Polos for mum.

Behind the counter, the shelves along the wall were chock-a-block with huge jars of sweets that you bought by

A 1954 magazine advert for the popular Spangles fruit-flavoured sweets.

weight, usually two ounces at a time, but a quarter pound if you were flush with money. There were hundreds of different sweets: pear drops, aniseed balls, Kola Kubes, sweet peanuts, sugar almonds, nut brittle, fruit bonbons, sherbet lemons, milk gums, jelly babies, jelly beans, dolly mixtures, American Hard Gums, Liquorice Allsorts, chocolate honeycomb, marshmallows, and loads more! There was always the temptation to buy a thruppenny Lucky Bag, but they were expensive and all you got was a few sweets and a plastic toy. Sometimes there would be a box of toffee apples on the counter, but they wouldn't last long!

On hot summer days, the best treat would be a frozen Jubbly, which was frozen orange juice in an unusual triangular-shaped carton. You would tear one corner of the carton and suck the frozen orange juice like a lolly, but without a lollystick. As you held the carton in your warm hands, the orange juice would start to melt into the bottom, which allowed you to turn the carton up and drink the juice through the hole in the top corner. It took ages to finish a Jubbly, much longer than a lolly, and they were very refreshing.

Bonfire Night

Most children vaguely knew that Bonfire Night was the annual remembrance of Guy Fawkes' failed gunpowder plot to blow up the Houses of Parliament in London. They may not have known that it happened as long ago as 1605, but they knew it was on the fifth of November. As with most historical events, its significance was completely lost on the minds of kids who were only interested in joining the excitement of a festive atmosphere. Once the dark evenings of autumn arrived, there was little opportunity to have fun playing outside, and this Guy Fawkes event allowed kids to legitimately do things that would normally be frowned upon, like making bonfires and handling fireworks. Many kids started planning for Bonfire Night well in advance; collecting and storing wood and other flammable materials as far back as September, in the last few days of their school summer holiday. You would spend the whole weekend before Bonfire Night making an effigy of Guy Fawkes to look as real as possible, stuffed with newspapers and dressed in old clothes with a football for a head and a paper face mask. Eventually the Guy would be burned on top of a big bonfire on the night itself, but in the days leading up to 5 November, you needed to earn, or beg, some money to pay for your fireworks. The Guy would be dragged around to some busy street corner, market, pub, railway or tube station, where it would be leant up against a wall or some railings, and then you and your mates would pester passers-by to give you a 'penny for the Guy!' Sometimes kids would forgo the making of a dummy Guy and instead would take turns in dressing themselves up as the Guy, complete with Guy Fawkes face mask, and sit slumped on the pavement while their mates cadged money from people in the street. This was very dangerous because disgruntled passers-by and mischief-makers would sometimes kick the Guy as they went past, and so the penny-beggars would need to stand close by to protect their friend from harm. Most people got paid weekly, and so Thursday and Friday nights were the best nights to go out cadging a 'penny for the Guy!' Once

This 1950s advert for Standard Fireworks captures a typical schoolboy's excitement on Bonfire Night.

the handouts started to dry up and the cold began to set into your bones, you and your mates would drag your 'Guy' off to home turf and share out your earnings.

The fireworks would normally be bought on the night itself, as most mums wouldn't allow them to be brought into the house – what with all those open coal fires! Kids bought fireworks and matches from shops with ease because there were no restrictions in place then. Most of your money would be spent on penny bangers, and you might buy the odd Roman candle, Catherine wheel, jumping cracker and rocket. Some of these could be unreliable and you didn't want to risk your money on expensive fireworks when there was no certainty that they would work. Many a blue touch paper was lit, only to burn down to its end and fizzle out, leaving you staring at it from a distance. Mischievous boys could cause a lot of trouble on Bonfire Night by misusing fireworks in various dangerous ways, such as tying a bunch of bangers together to get one big boom, lighting Catherine wheels on the ground so that they went out of control, or throwing lighted jumping crackers near the girls to frighten them. Worst of all, penny bangers were chucked all over the place and you never knew when one was going to come flying past your nose! The lead-up to Bonfire Night was an adventure and the night itself was exciting, but it was also a dirty, frightening, dangerous and smelly night, with the horrible smell of sulphur and the air filled with dirty smoke from bonfires. The noise from the exploding fireworks and screaming girls was only broken by the sound of fire engine and ambulance bells. Meanwhile, mums everywhere were praying for rain!

Remember, remember, the fifth of November,

The Gunpowder, Treason and Plot,

I can think of no reason

Why the Gunpowder Treason

Should ever be forgot.

Too Old For Toys!

There came a time when you were too old for toys and games but too young to mix with the teenagers. You were confused about what generation you belonged to. It hit some kids earlier than others and sometimes led to the break-up of old childhood friendships. Often it happened around the time you changed schools, after your eleven-plus exam, which gave you the opportunity to make new friends. You lost interest in the old tried and tested ways of passing the time and sought out new interests. You got bored with catching tadpoles in the local pond and you wanted a fishing rod so you could do proper fishing. On a wet day, instead of wandering around Woolworths with your mates, as you used to do, you found yourself sitting in a record booth at your local record shop listening to the latest Everly Brothers' hit. Instead of being dragged reluctantly around the shops and street markets by your mum, you became a more willing shopper and even started to take notice of what the shops and stalls were selling. Girls stopped doing handstands up against the wall and wanted rid of their little girlie ribbons. They began to take an interest in teenage fashions and reading mum's magazines. Boys cringed at any public show of affection

Two young boys play football in the middle of a central London street in 1951. Note that there is no traffic or parked cars around.

from their parents; quickly moving their head away at the first sight of their mum's lips approaching their cheek for a goodbye kiss.

You would start using trendy teenage words like 'cool', 'cat', and 'square'. Instead of hanging-out with your mates on someone's doorstep, you and your friends would be more likely to gather in the local coffee-bar and listen to the latest records on the jukebox, sharing one bottle of Coca-Cola between five! You might go to the local church youth club to play table tennis and listen to records. You would even find yourself listening with more interest to the doorstep banter between grown-ups. It was a confusing time when you were sort of playing at being a teenager.

It was a time for trying new grown-up things. Sadly, it was often at the tender age of just ten or eleven that many kids were tempted to try their first puff on a cigarette. A lot were sick and never touched a fag again, but for many it was their first step to a lifetime of smoking. Smoking was advertised as a cool and sophisticated thing to do. There was never any mention of it being unhealthy!

Whereas you used just to shovel food into your mouth to fill your empty stomach and boost your energy levels, you began to develop a taste for food and even enjoy the experience of eating your favourite dishes. There were few takeaway food shops back then but there were plenty of places in the high streets and marketplaces where you could savour your best-loved local dishes. From traditional Lancashire hotpot to Welsh cawl, to Londoners' pie and mash with liquor, tripe and onions, and jellied eels – we all had our personal favourite.

Boys frequently took more interest in supporting their local football team and going to the matches with their dad. All of a sudden, you found that you were growing up and fast approaching your teenage years, and the onset of all those hormonal issues.

Four

GAMES, HOBBIES AND PASTIMES

Kids of every generation suffer boredom if they are not kept occupied. In the 1950s, although all the best fun was reserved for outside the house, there was a host of tried and tested pastimes to keep you busy at home in the evenings.

Everyone had his or her own favourite indoor hobby, and many children got drawn into collecting something or other. Stamp collecting was very popular and was usually a shared interest between friends, who would swap stamps between each other to make up sets or get rid of ones they already had. There was always the thrill of seeing an unusual stamp and the anticipation that it could be valuable. Someone always seemed to know someone else's dad that had a Stanley Gibbons stamp catalogue to check if a stamp was rare or not. Most kids were very aware of what their stamp collection was worth, usually only a few shillings. Often the stamp-collecting book was worth more than the collection it held, but collecting was addictive and interesting, and once you started you were hooked. Children often learned more about the geography of the world from stamp collecting than they did through schoolwork.

With limited access to telephones, picture postcards were still regularly sent though the post to pass messages between friends and family. Postcard collecting was a cost-free hobby that many children took up. From Matchbox and Dinky Toys to marbles, there were loads of things to collect and swap with your mates.

Most children had a secret box of treasures in which they kept all their most valued little possessions. Usually a small wooden or tin box, preferably one of those black tin moneyboxes with a key so that it could be safely locked up. You would inspect its contents as often as you could, just to make sure that everything was still there, and possibly add another unique piece to your treasure trove of collectables: an old bus ticket, a favourite coloured marble, your membership card for The Biggles Club, a small picture of Doris Day from a discarded newspaper, a cigarette picture card of Stanley Matthews, a small unknown key, and perhaps some old Halfpenny or Farthing coins. Worthless junk they might be, but these were often the prized possessions of a young child.

Model making was very popular and children usually didn't need any encouragement to make things out of whatever materials were to hand. Depending on how well off your parents were, you could mould something with plasticine for next to nothing, or you could buy the latest Airfix model or Meccano construction kit. Mind you, Airfix and Meccano were usually only of interest to the boys, as

This 1958 magazine advert for Croid glue captures a 1950s family scene with each member of the family enjoying a hobby. Typically, dad is dressed in shirt and tie and smoking a pipe, but at least he has rolled his sleeves up to appear casual.

were toy soldiers and messing around with chemistry sets. Girls were much more inclined to mimic their mum's activities, and mums were usually keen to teach them skills like sewing, knitting, embroidery and baking cakes. These were all jobs that were considered to be essential for girls to learn for when they grew up and became homemakers, but they were also very popular hobbies, and girls were very keen students.

Children were very good at finding things to do for free, like scrap-booking, tracing and drawing pictures. A few sheets of old newspaper could be made into all sorts of shapes and objects, and pretty soon you would become

RADIO IS THE HOBBY WITH THE FUTURE

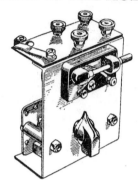

Start learning by building this **D5 Crystal Set:-** D5 Coil with complete blue prints, circuit drawings and instructions **5/-**. Full kit of parts **15/-**. Built ready to play **18/-**. All parts supplied separately. Receives long and medium waves.

**Hillfields Mail Radio,
8 Burnham Road,
Whitley, Coventry**

This crystal radio kit advert from 1950 is aimed at young boys, but the kit is not cheap at 15/- (15 shillings), equivalent to about £19 at today's values based on the retail price index.

SUBBUTEO

HERE IS A FOOTBALL GAME WHERE VICTORY OR DEFEAT DEPENDS UPON THE SKILL OF THE PLAYER INSTEAD OF BY THE SHAKE OF A DICE OR BY THE TURN OF A CARD

THE GAME OF "TABLE SOCCER"

THE REPLICA OF ASSOCIATION FOOTBALL

COLOURS OF ALL LEAGUE CLUBS AVAILABLE

NO

DICE ... BLOWING ...

CARDS ... OR BOARD

Played with 22 miniature men, ball and goals. All the thrills of real Football! Dribbling, corner and penalty kicks, offside, goal saves, injuries, &c.

★ PRICE **10/7** INCLUDING PURCHASE TAX AND POSTAGE

or send stamp for full details and Order form to:—

P. A. ADOLPH, 30 The Lodge, Langton Green, Tunbridge Wells
KENT

This magazine advert from 1950 offers the Subbuteo table soccer game, with miniature players in the colours of any football league club, at a price of 10/7 (ten shillings and seven pence), equivalent to about £14 at today's values based on the retail price index.

something of an origami expert. It wasn't unusual for a child to sit alone at a table and play games for long periods at a time. A jigsaw puzzle, bagatelle, perhaps a card game like Patience, or even a couple of small magnets could keep a child busy for ages. Young ones occupied themselves by playing at being grown-ups, using such things as toy tea sets and miniature toolboxes. Of course, there was always plenty of time for girls to play with their dolls and the doll's house that was probably made by dad. Not forgetting all the dressing-up games, complete with make-up and mum's frock and high heels.

All the boys wanted to have a Hornby Dublo electric train set, but to most it was just a dream and you had to make do with the more primitive and less expensive wind-up toy train. Girls weren't allowed near electric train sets; these were definitely within the boys' domain. Then again, even boys sometimes struggled to get control of their Hornby train set if dad was around!

There were many indoor hobbies and pastimes that were equally popular with both boys and girls. Lots of children had pen pals that they would regularly write to. Newspapers, magazines and comics would often have pen pal columns listing children that were looking for pen pals living in certain areas. You could have a pen pal that lived in another city or county, or even in another country! As with stamp collecting, this was a great way to learn geography as well as gaining knowledge of how people lived in other places.

There were loads of children's books, annuals and comics to read; favourite books included anything by Enid Blyton or Beatrix Potter, and other books like *Heidi, Black Beauty,*

Treasure Island, *Winnie-the-Pooh* and *The Chronicles of Narnia*. Boys were keen readers of *Billy Bunter of Greyfriars School*, *Just William*, and the Biggles series of books. Everyone equally enjoyed reading Enid Blyton's adventures of *The Famous Five*.

The most popular comics and annuals included *The Beano*, *The Dandy*, *Topper*, *Eagle*, *Wizard*, *Beezer*, *Tiger* (including 'Roy of The Rovers'), *Hotspur*, *Lion*, *Girl* and *Bunty*. Some of the favourite comic strips included 'The Bash Street Kids', 'Lord Snooty', 'Keyhole Kate' and 'Dan Dare'. There were so many comics around that you would normally only buy one or two and then swap with your mates so that you could keep up with all your comic strip heroes. Many of the comics produced a large annual each year, and one or two of these would usually find their way onto your Christmas wish list. While everyone enjoyed the *Rupert Bear* annuals, essential reading for the girls was the *School Friend Annual* and the *Girls' Crystal Annual*.

Whole families would often wile away the evening playing card games like Snap, Old Maid, Fish, Rummy and Pontoon (sometimes called Twenty-one). Board games were also very popular, with favourites like Monopoly, Cluedo, Snakes and Ladders, Scrabble and Lotto (sometimes called Housey Housey), which was similar to Bingo. Dominoes and Crib (Cribbage) were also regularly played, as were games that enabled you to pit your wits against one other person, like Noughts and Crosses, Battleships, Draughts and Chess. These were all well-liked and encouraged by mum and dad because they kept you quiet – that is, until someone cheated!

When you got bored with all this mental activity, you could always suggest that mum and dad join you in a game of hide and seek. Do you remember carefully hiding yourself in the back of that cupboard for what seemed like ages, and then that awful feeling when you realised they had forgotten you? You eventually came out to find mum and dad dozing in front of the fire, and they hadn't been looking for you at all!

In good weather, you would often play board games outside, either on a patch of grass or on one another's doorsteps. You steadily progressed from Tiddlywinks to Monopoly, which was always a firm favourite with kids. Card games like Brag, Cheat, Cribbage, Pontoon, Rummy, Snap and Whist were also regularly played on doorsteps or in passageways. Football and cricket were forever being played in the street, in open spaces or bomb ruins, but there were loads of other cost-free street games and activities to keep you occupied. Many of these were group games, and before you could start playing, you had to choose someone to be 'it'!

In street games, 'it' was the term used to describe the person who was designated to seek out, find, chase or catch the other kids in the game. If someone suggested playing a hide-and-seek or chase game then he or she would own that one game for its duration. A lot of these games required someone to be 'it'. To pick who would be 'it', the person that suggested the game would recite the words of a rhyme while 'dipping' (pointing at each person in turn). The long version of this would eliminate people one by one until there was only one person left, and that person would then be 'it'. In the short version it would simply be the person pointed to on the last word of the rhyme that would be 'it'. There were loads of different rhymes, with lots of rude and politically incorrect versions. Here are a couple of the innocent ones:

Ip-dip sky-blue who's-it? Not you!

Eeny, Meeny, Miny, Mo!
Catch a tiger by the toe!
If he hollers let him go!
Eeny, Meeny. Miny, Mo!

You're It!

There were hundreds of street games with all sorts of variations being played in different parts of the country. Here are a few to jog the memory and remind you of all those times you crossed your fingers and shouted 'fainites!' when playing these games.

Blind Man's Buff: One person was chosen to be 'it', and he or she was then blindfolded and turned around three times to disorientate him or her. The player who was 'it' then tried to catch hold of one of the players and guess who it was by touching their face and hair. If 'it' couldn't guess who it was, then he or she would let go of that player and try to catch another player, repeating the process until a player's name was guessed and then that player became 'it'.

Boatman Boatman, Farmer Farmer (the younger kids' version of British Bulldogs): One person was chosen to be 'it' and became the boatman. The boatman stood in the middle of a pre-agreed play area and all the other players stood on a line at one edge. The players then chanted, 'Boatman,

Children's books, magazines and games kept children occupied on cold winter evenings in the 1950s.

Boatman, can we cross the river?' The boatman replied, 'You can only cross the river if you are wearing (name of a colour).' Any player wearing something of that colour then crossed freely to the other side of the play area. The players that were not wearing the required colour had to run to the other side without being caught by the boatman. Any players that were caught then joined the boatman as catchers, and the game was repeated until there was only one uncaught player left and he or she was the winner.

British Bulldogs, Bulldog, Bullies, Red Rover, Runno: Any number of boys and girls would join in to play this, but it was not for the faint-hearted; this game would usually result in a few injuries, particularly when played on a hard surface or if played by mixed age groups. The favoured places to play this were in fields and on bomb ruin sites. To start with, one or two players were selected to be bulldogs and they were made to stand in the middle of the field. There were two safe areas on opposite side edges of the field. All of the non-bulldogs gathered in one of these safe areas. The main objective of the game was for the non-bulldogs to run across the field from one safe area to the other without being caught by the bulldogs. The game started with one of the bulldogs naming a player that was to be the first to attempt the run from one side to the other, and the bulldogs would then attempt to catch the runner. If he or she was caught by a bulldog then the bulldog had to hold onto the failed runner and shout 'British Bulldog; one, two, three!' The caught runner then became a bulldog. If he or she did reach the other side without being caught then they were deemed to be in the safe area and could not be caught. Once the runner had either been caught or reached the safe area then all the other non-bulldogs had to immediately attempt to cross the playing area themselves (this was called the 'rush' or 'bullrush'), with the bulldogs trying to catch as many as possible using the same rules as before. Once all the surviving non-bulldogs had reached the 'safe' area on the other side of the field, the rush began again to get across the field in the opposite direction, avoiding the bulldogs. The game continued until all the players had become bulldogs, and the winner was the last person to be caught. It was quite difficult to catch someone and hold onto them for enough time to shout 'British Bulldog; one, two, three!' It usually needed some tough rugby tackling, which resulted in grubby and torn clothes, and countless bruises, cuts and grazes. As with other games, various versions were played around the country with other local names being used to describe it.

Bumps: Not so much a game as an endurance test or punishment on your birthday. It could be quite dangerous and so it was usually only performed on boys. Girls sometimes did their own gentle version. It entailed the birthday boy or girl being held spread-eagle by their arms and legs, and lifted up and down in the air whilst their mates counted the number of birthday years, hitting or bumping their bum against the floor, once for each year.

Cartwheels: This activity was mostly done by girls, but boys enjoyed it too. It involved the girl first standing upright and throwing herself sideways onto one outstretched arm; then the other until her whole body had turned a full 360 degrees and she was back on her feet again. In motion, the arms and legs took the shape of a cartwheel's spokes. Any opportunity to show the boys those navy blue knickers!

Children would sometimes build up collections of favourite comics and books.

Cat's Cradle: A game for two people, usually girls, to create a series of patterns, including the 'cat's cradle', out of a loop of string wrapped around the fingers and wrists. Individual girls, sometimes with the use of their teeth, fashioned simpler creations, like a 'cup and saucer'.

Conkers: The game was played by two children, each with a conker threaded onto a piece of string or an old shoelace. One player would let the conker dangle on the full length of the string while the other player swung their conker to hit it. The players took turns to strike each other's conker until one broke. Sometimes it was the attacking conker that broke. The conkers were given names to identify their worth; a new conker was called a 'none-er', and when a 'none-er' broke another 'none-er' it became a 'one-er', then a 'two-er', 'three-er', and so on. The winning conker inherited the previous score of the losing conker as well as gaining the score from that particular game. So if a 'two-er' beat a 'three-er' then the winning conker became a 'six-er'. The hardest conkers usually won but there was a lot of cheating, with players using various methods to aid the hardening of their conkers, including soaking them in vinegar overnight, baking them in the oven for a short time, and seasoning them by keeping them for a year before use.

Egg, Egga, Bad Egg (played with a tennis ball): The person who was 'it' would give the players a subject like colours or football teams to choose a name from. The players would huddle together to whisper and choose names. One of the players would then call out loud all of the names chosen by the players. The person who was 'it' would then throw the ball high into the air or against a wall and shout out one of the names (i.e. blue or Arsenal), and the player that had chosen that name would have to catch or retrieve the ball while the others ran away. Once the person had retrieved the ball, he or she would shout 'Stop!' or 'Egg!', or something similar, and the players would have to stand still. The person with the ball could then take up to three giant steps towards any of the scattered players, and throw the ball at that person. If the ball hit the target then he or she would become 'it' and a new game would begin. If the thrower missed then he would be 'it'.

Five Stones (known to me as 'Gobs'): This game was often played on doorsteps and involved five evenly sized small stones and one larger stone, with the player using just one hand. One person would play at a time by placing one of the small stones on the back of his or her hand and throwing it into the air, picking up the larger stone and catching the thrown stone on its way down. This was repeated, adding one small stone to the back of the hand at each throw until all five small stones had been thrown into the air and caught at the same time as picking up the large stone. Your turn ended if you dropped any of the stones or failed to pick up the large stone before the small stones were caught in the palm of your hand. In an alternative version, you would throw the five small stones onto the ground and place the large stone on the back of your hand. You would then throw the large stone in the air and pick up one small stone from the ground before catching the large stone on its way down. You would continue to pick up one stone at a time until you had all five small stones and the one large stone in the palm of your hand. This was called 'onsies'. If you were successful then you would start again with five small stones on the ground, but this time pick up to two small stones at a time (called 'twosies'). If you continued to be successful then you would then progress to 'threesies', 'foursies' and 'fifesies'. You were allowed to throw the large stone up from the back of your hand and sweep the small stones on the ground together with your fingers, but if you used this tactic then you had to catch the large stone on the back of your hand in between each sweep.

French Skipping (also known as Elastics): This was a girl's game, played using a very long piece of knicker elastic tied into a loop. Two or more girls would stand inside the loop of elastic, a few feet apart, with the elastic stretched around the outside of their ankles. The first player would then perform a series of skipping movements on, under, and over the elastic. Both feet under the elastic, both feet on top of the elastic, one on top and one under, one on top and one under and then swap feet. The player would then move around one girl to the next section of elastic and repeat the skipping movement. The skips or jumps were often done in time to a skipping rhyme. If the player successfully completed a round of jumps without tripping over or making a mistake, then the elastic would be moved up to knee level (called 'knee-sies'), then thigh level ('thigh-sies'), and then waist level ('waist-sies'). The player would be out if she failed to do the correct jump, and then one of the others would come out from the elastic to have a go.

Frisbees: Throwing disc-shaped objects was always a popular outdoor sport, but when the Wham-O toy company in America launched this special flying disc in 1957, it became a proper throwing and catching game for kids. The Frisbee was also thrown for dogs to run, jump and catch in mid-air.

Handstands: This was an activity done by both boys and girls. Starting from an upright position with arms out-stretched above the head, the person would bend forward and sort of tumble themselves forward onto the palms of their hands so that balancing on their hands supported their upturned body. The handstand would be complete when their body was held straight with arms and legs fully extended. Sometimes handstands would be done free-standing and sometimes up against a wall, finishing with the soles of the feet resting against the wall. Girls would tuck the hem of their skirt into the elasticated leg of their navy blue knickers to maintain their modesty while performing handstands.

He, It, Tag, Tig, Tip: Known by various names, this was the simplest and most basic game of chase for a group of kids to play. The person chosen to be 'it' ran around trying to touch or 'tag' one of the others. When touched or tagged then that person became 'it' until he or she touched another player. You could avoid being 'tagged' by lifting your feet off the ground temporarily by pulling yourself up onto a wall or a bar so that your feet dangled just above the ground. There were loads of optional rules for this game.

He Ball: Similar game to He, It, Tag, Tig and Tip except with 'He Ball' the person that was 'it' chased the other players with a ball. If 'it' managed to throw the ball and hit a player then that player would become 'it'.

Hopscotch: Usually played in the street. A set of eight or ten equally sized joined–up squares was chalked onto the pavement in a hopscotch pattern and each square was then numbered. The first player would stand behind the starting line and toss a stone into square number 'one' and then hop over square 'one' and land in square 'two' on one leg, then continue hopping through the hopscotch, landing on one leg in single squares and two legs in double squares. At the end you would turn around and make your way back down through the hopscotch until you reached the square number 'two'. You would then bend down and pick up the stone from square number 'one', hop into square 'one' and back to the start again. You then threw the stone into square number 'two' and repeated the hopping process as before

Girls and boys each had their own preferred 'must-read' comics and annuals.

only this time hopping over square number 'two' as you made your way through the hopscotch. You repeated this through all the numbered squares, always hopping over the square with the stone in it. A player was deemed to be out if the stone failed to land within the lines of the correct square, he or she stepped into the square where the stone was, put two feet down in a single box, stepped on any of the chalked lines, or lost his or her balance while bending over to pick up the stone. If you managed to complete the whole hopscotch successfully then you hopped through the whole hopscotch again without a stone in any box, and out the top of the hopscotch to finish.

Hula hoop: The hula hoop craze hit Britain in 1958 with the arrival of the American Wham-O toy company's lightweight tubular plastic hoop, made from a recently invented durable plastic, and called the hula hoop. It was a toy hoop that you twirled around your waist, limbs or neck for as long as possible, and you had competitions between friends to see who could keep it going for the longest time. It was most popular with the girls, and grown-up women also enjoyed it as a way to keep fit. It was a short-lived craze that only lasted for a few months. Wham-O relaunched the hula hoop in the late 1960s.

Jacks: This game was very similar to Five Stones except it was played using a small bouncy rubber ball or a table tennis ball, and between five and ten small stones. You would bounce the ball once and pick up stones, catching the ball before it bounced again. As with Five Stones, you played 'onesies', 'twosies', 'threesies', 'foursies', 'fifesies', 'sixies' etc., but again, there were several versions to the game.

Kiss Chase: There never seemed to be any rules to this 'it' game. Girls chased after boys to kiss them, and the boys ran away. If the girls caught a boy and kissed him then he would be 'it' and he would have to chase the girls for a kiss, but it never seemed to happen like that. The boys were always running away – although they did slow down a bit when they got to about ten or eleven years old!

Knock Down Ginger: A game that was mainly played after dark and could get you into serious trouble with your mum and dad. In its simplest form, you knocked on street doors and ran away without being seen. Everyone had knockers on their street doors in the 1950s. More advanced players would quietly tie cotton to a street door knocker and then reel the cotton out to the other side of the street, where you would hide and then pull the cotton until it broke, thus lifting the knocker and dropping it back in place to create a loud knock on the door. Sometimes you would do three or four knockers at the same time, but that was risky because there was more of a chance that one of the victims might come out and chase after you.

Leapfrog: Players vaulted over each other's stooped backs. There could be any number of players. The first player stooped and the second player vaulted over him or her. On landing, that player also stooped, a few feet in front of the first stooped player. Then the third player vaulted over each of the two stooped players. The game continued like this with each player joining the line of stooped players. Once all of the players were stooped then the first player stood up and vaulted over all of the other players, and so on.

Lolly Sticks: Played with a bunch of used flat wooden lolly sticks. The lolly sticks were held a few inches above the ground and dropped into a heap. You then picked up all of the sticks that weren't touching any of the others and used one of these to move or flick each stick off the pile without moving any of the others. If you moved another stick while flicking then one of the other players started a new game. The winner was the player who had picked up the most sticks during their turn.

Marbles: There were many different versions of Marbles and usually the rules were agreed before the game started. In its simplest form, players took turns to roll or flick

The Beano and *The Dandy* were the two best-known and most popular 'must-read' comics for both girls and boys – all those fabulous comic strip characters, like Dennis the Menace, The Bash Street Kids, and Desperate Dan – just to mention a few.

their marbles at their opponents' marbles, and if they hit one then that marble became theirs. Sometimes the game was played within an agreed area or circle, in which case you had to flick your marbles from the edge of the circle without encroaching. The aim was to either hit one of your opponents' marbles that had already been placed near the centre of the circle at the start of the game, or to knock one of their marbles out of the circle. If you were successful then your 'shooter' marble remained where it had stopped and you could shoot again from that spot. If you were unsuccessful then the next player began his or her go from outside the circle. Loads of different versions and rules!

Roller Skating: In the 1950s, children's roller skates were still quite primitive. They were simply four ball-bearing metal wheels attached to a foot-shaped flat piece of metal. You put your foot onto the flat metal plate, with your heel pressed against a small ridge at the back. There was a leather strap attached to the back of the skates, which you would wrap around your instep to hold the skates on. At the front, there was an adjustable metal grip on each side, and you tightened these against your shoe to hold the front of your shoe in place. They were absolutely useless! Impossible to keep attached for more than a few minutes at a time. You would often see a lone skate hurtling down the road having escaped its wearer, and sometimes the skate would still have a shoe attached to it! Lots of twisted ankles and grazed knees, but you always went back to have another go!

Run Outs: The person that was 'it' would close his or her eyes and count to an agreed number, usually between ten and one hundred, while the players ran and hid. 'It' would then go in search of the players and each one he found would join him to search for the remaining hidden players. The players could change their hiding place during the game as long as they weren't seen by any of the searchers. The last player to be found would be the winner. Seekers would often call out the names of hidden players in the hope that they would answer, and sometimes they did!

Scissors, Paper, Stone: A simple game that was usually played to determine who was to go first in a game, or who was 'it', or who should do a dare. Best played with up to three people, but when played with more than two people there were lots of drawn games, which meant playing again. Being a very fast game, you sometimes played best of three. The players would form a circle and each player would hold out their arm and make a loose fist. You would then shake your fist up and down counting 'one-two-three' and on the downward stroke of 'three' you would open your fist to reveal either a 'scissors' – two fingers open, 'paper' – flat open hand, or 'stone' - clenched fist. The winner would be determined as follows:

Scissors cuts Paper – Scissors wins
Paper wraps Stone – Paper wins
Stone blunts Scissors – Stone wins

Skipping (with rope): Very popular, mainly played by girls and usually done in time to a skipping rhyme. A skipping rope, often adapted from mum's washing line, was never too far away to bring into use when someone suggested it. Girls would often skip alone but it was best played as a group competition. Depending upon the number of players, the rope would be turned by one girl at either end, or one girl would turn the rope with the other end tied to a lamppost. The turners get the rope to slap the pavement in time to a skipping rhyme being chanted by the skippers. There were loads of rhymes with key words and phrases that prompted the skipper to do a trick in one turn of the rope; like jumping extra high with both feet together, hopping the rope very close to the ground, kicking one foot out, crossing and uncrossing feet and legs, and turning to face the other way. Boys were always fascinated by the skill of the girls and the tricks they could do. The skipper would run out from the turning rope, around one of the girls twirling it, and back in time to the beat of the skipping rope hitting the pavement. Certain phrases in the rhymes would invite other girls to join in with, or to take over from, the skipper on the next turn of the rope. Double Dutch was really difficult, with two turning ropes for the skipper to negotiate. There were names for all the tricks, like Kick (kicking one foot out), Sizzler (crossing and uncrossing feet) and Split (opening legs wide apart). There were so many skipping variations and so many rhymes, with several different versions adapted around the country.

Tin Tan Tommy: Played with an old tin can. One person was chosen to be 'it' and a place was designated to be the 'home' point, where the tin can would sit while the game was played. To start the game, one of the players would throw the tin can as hard as he or she could away from the home point. Whoever was 'it' would chase after the can to retrieve it and return it to 'home'. Meanwhile, all the others would run and hide. Once the can was back in place on the 'home' spot, the person who was 'it' would go and search for the other players. When one was discovered, 'it' would run back to the can and bash it up and down on the ground while shouting 'Tin Tan Tommy, I see Mickey behind the wall', or something similar. But if the discovered person could get back to the can and bash it on the ground before 'it', then he or she was 'home' and safe, otherwise that person became 'it' and another game began.

Two-Balls (juggling with tennis balls): A girls' game that was usually played by juggling with two balls in the air or against a wall, but sometimes the girls would use three or four balls. It was a skill that was mastered by most girls at a very young age, and although boys admired the skills, they saw it as a girl's game and usually steered clear of it. Playing two-balls was always done to the beat of a chanted rhyme. There were lots of tricks that were described with words like plainsy, upsy, over, dropsy, bouncy, legsy, twirly. Such words were inserted in the rhymes to indicate when to do a certain movement with a ball … One, two, three and PLAINSY; four, five, six and PLAINSY …

> Over the garden wall
> I let my baby sister fall;
> My mother came out
> And gave me a clout,
> I told my mother
> Not to boss me about;
> She gave me another
> To match the other,
> Over the garden wall.

Juggling two balls against the pavement was usually done to the rhyme *One Two Three O'Leary*.

Up the Wall: Usually played with cigarette cards or other collecting cards from packets of Barrett's sweets or Brooke Bond Tea cards. Teenagers sometimes played it with coins (farthings, halfpennies and pennies). From an agreed spot, a few feet away from a wall, you would flick your card or coin forwards as accurately as possible. The player who got nearest the wall won and took all the cards or coins already along the ground.

What's the Time Mr Wolf?: One person was chosen to be 'it' and a place was designated to be the 'home' point. The player who was 'it' was called Mr Wolf (sometimes Mr Fox or Mr Bear), and would either stand with his or her back to the other players or be walking slowly away from them. The players would slowly creep up on Mr Wolf chanting, 'What's the time Mr Wolf?' The wolf would stop, turn around and reply, 'It's one o'clock'. The players would continue to ask, 'What's the time Mr Wolf?' and the wolf would reply, 'it's two o'clock', 'three o'clock', until eventually the wolf would reply with a growl, 'It's DINNERTIME!' Mr Wolf would then chase the other players who had to try to run back to the 'home' point without being caught. The first person to be caught became Mr Wolf.

Yo-yo: Various adaptations of the yo-yo have been around for centuries, but the modern yo-yo was only developed in the 1930s, and remained popular throughout the '50s. Basically, it was a toy consisting of two equally sized and weighted small discs connected with an axle, and with a long piece of string tied around the axle. The rest of the string was wound around this axle until only the end piece, tied in the shape of a loop, was still showing. The end of the string was looped around the player's forefinger, and the player performed various skilful tricks with the yo-yo by rotating it along the full length of the string. A very skilful game, with lots of tricks, often played as a competition among friends. Sometimes there were yo-yo competitions held during Saturday Morning Pictures at the local cinemas.

Five

ENTERTAINMENT, MUSIC AND FASHION

Sandwiched between the horrors of the Second World War and the excitement of the Swinging Sixties, the 1950s was a period of calm but also a time of exhilarating new experiences in entertainment, music and fashion that would start to prepare 1950s kids for the revolutionary changes that would be part of their teenage years. In the early 1950s, Britain saw the arrival of 'rock and roll' music and teen films from America, and for the first time ever, you witnessed teenagers being arrested for dancing in the aisles at the local cinemas. You had your first experience of the great theatre musicals and saw all of your Wild West cowboy heroes on the big screen. Horror and science fiction films became very popular, as did science fiction comics. The first drip-dry, non-iron clothes made from synthetic materials went on sale, and Levi jeans became trendy for the first time. Teenage girls tried to outdo each other with their backcombed bouffant and beehive hairstyles, and they celebrated the introduction of the long-awaited seamless nylon stockings, while boys delighted in the newly arrived bikini two-piece swimsuit for girls!

Television sets replaced the radio as the most popular form of home entertainment in working-class homes, and you saw the first TV adventure series, sitcoms and quiz shows. You had your first glimpse of the new British fashion revolution in 1955 when Mary Quant opened her first fashion boutique, Bazaar, on London's King's Road. The British pop music revolution was already well under way with pop stars like Cliff Richard, Adam Faith, Tommy Steele, Lonnie Donegan and Shirley Bassey having their first number one hit singles in the UK charts. It was back in 1958 that John Lennon, Paul McCartney and George Harrison first played together in 'The Quarrymen' skiffle group, little knowing the huge influence they would later have in worldwide popular music culture as The Beatles.

In 1959, the British Motor Corporation launched the Mini, which was later to become a big fashion icon. It was in that same year that you first heard music produced by the Tamla Record Company, which quickly changed its name to the now familiar 'Motown'. The hula hoop and frisbee plastic toys arrived from America in 1958, and the hula hoop became a great keep-fit activity for young women looking to maintain the tiny waistline that was needed to conform to the figure-hugging flared and pencil skirt fashions of the era.

It was in the 1950s that the term 'teenager' first came into use to describe young people of the 'teen' years. Prior to

Expresso Bongo was Cliff Richard's second film appearance during 1959, the first being *Serious Charge*. Both films featured music performed by Cliff Richard and the newly renamed Shadows, previously known as The Drifters.

that, adolescents were simply called young people, boys and girls, or youths. It bridged the gap between kids and adults, and gave them their own identity.

Having experienced Britain's years of post-war austerity, the 1950s baby-boomers had modest expectations of leisure and enjoyment. They revelled in every new experience of music and entertainment, and watched from a distance as teenage and adult fashions evolved. There was no computer-generated imagery, stadium-filled pop concerts, or chains of kids' fashion shops to feast on. Instead, children growing up in the 1950s would be left with their memories of the simple pleasures of childhood.

Cinema (Going to the Pictures)

If you were lucky enough to live anywhere near a cinema then you must have experienced the great joy of going to Saturday Morning Pictures. Two or three hundred unruly children would descend upon unsuspecting cinema commissionaires every Saturday morning for two or three hours of film and live variety entertainment. There were no grown-ups, just kids up to the age of about twelve or thirteen, and it was the absolute highlight of any week. You will probably remember the cinema manager having to stop the film and threaten to send you all home if you didn't behave, or booing when the screen went blank while the projectionist was changing reels. The solitary usherette would run for cover! It was controlled mayhem, with the stalls and circle areas filled with kids cheering for the goodies and booing the baddies. There were lots of short films, mainly westerns that seemed to consist of endless chases on horseback. The daring adventures of The Lone Ranger and Zorro, and the slapstick comedy of Mr Pastry would feature every week. And then there were the classic Charlie Chaplin and Buster Keaton films that had everyone in fits of laughter. And who can forget those wonderful old Shirley Temple films. During the film interval there would be all sorts of competitions, from yo-yo, hula hoop and juggling contests, to singing and dancing, and even competitions for the best skiffle group, with knock-out rounds each week leading to the grand final. Most cinemas had their own club, especially the large cinema chains, and you would have a club badge and be made to sing the club song each week. Whether you belonged to the ABC Minors, Empire Rangers or the Granadiers Club, you definitely will have enjoyed every minute you spent at Saturday Morning Pictures.

Going to the pictures was everyone's favourite outing. It enabled the young and old to climb out of their normal humdrum lifestyles and step into a fantasy world of adventure, comedy and romance. There was a distinct difference between the British-made films, which were generally down-to-earth, and the glitzy Hollywood movies that often portrayed everyone in America to be living in the lap of luxury. There were some great British films around in the 1950s, and a host of wonderful 'stiff-upper-lip' British film stars, like John Mills, Jack Hawkins, Kenneth More and Dirk Bogarde. They had all been making films since the 1930s, and were already household names, but seeing those very old 'silver screen' movies replayed in the 1950s endeared those film stars to a whole new generation.

Even if you were restricted to only the very occasional treat, you will surely have gone to see some of the best British war films ever made, like *The Cruel Sea* (1953), *The Dam Busters* (1954), *The Colditz Story* (1955), *Reach for the Sky* (1956) and *The Bridge Over the River Kwai* (1957). You can probably still whistle the 'Colonel Bogey March' without any prompting, and after all these years! You will also remember all those Ealing Studios comedy films, like *The Man in the White Suit* (1951), starring Alec Guinness,

Joan Greenwood and Cecil Parker. *The Lavender Hill Mob* (1951), starring Alec Guinness, Stanley Holloway, Sid James and Alfie Bass. *The Titfield Thunderbolt* (1952), starring Stanley Holloway, George Relph and John Gregson. And, *The Ladykillers* (1955), starring Alec Guinness, Herbert Lom and Peter Sellers. Other classic British comedy films included *The Happiest Days of Your Life* (1950), *The Belles of St Trinian's* (1954), *Doctor in the House* (1954), *Carry On Sergeant* (1958) and *I'm Alright Jack* (1959).

There were loads of marvellous British film actresses in the 1950s, including Claire Bloom, Diana Dors (d.1984), Margaret Leighton (d.1976), Margaret Rutherford (d.1972), Anna Neagle (d.1986), Jean Simmons, Glynis Johns, Joan Greenwood (d.1987), Audrey Hepburn (born in Brussels and grew up in Holland, but we think of her as being English) (d.1993), Dinah Sheridan, Petula Clark, Virginia McKenna, Edith Evans (d.1976), Phyllis Calvert (d.2002), Dorothy Tutin (d.2001), Ann Todd (d.1993), Celia Johnson (d.1982), Joan Collins, Kay Kendall (d.1959), Elizabeth Allan (d.1990), Joyce Grenfell (d.1979), Fay Compton (d.1978), Elizabeth Sellars, Margaret Lockwood (d.1990), Deborah Kerr (d.2007), Peggy Mount (d.2001), Dorothy Tutin (d.2001), Elizabeth Taylor, and Joan Sims (d.2001) – to name but a few.

And of course, a myriad of splendid British film actors that included Harry Andrews (d.1989), Richard Attenborough, George Baker, Stanley Baker (d.1976), Alfie Bass (d.1987), Dirk Bogarde (d.1999), Richard Burton (d.1984), Ian Carmichael, George Cole, Peter Cushing (d.1994), Michael Denison (d.1998), Robert Donat (d.1958), Denholm Elliott (d.1992), Peter Finch (d.1977), John

Gielgud (d.2000), Stewart Granger (d.1993), Cary Grant (d.1986), John Gregson (d.1975), Alec Guinness (d.2000), William Hartnell (d.1975), Laurence Harvey (d.1973), Jack Hawkins (d.1973), Richard Hearne (d.1979), Stanley Holloway (d.1982), Michael Hordern (d.1995), Trevor Howard (d.1988), Boris Karloff (d.1969), Charles Laughton (d.1962) Bernard Lee (d.1981), Christopher Lee, James Mason (d.1984), Michael Medwin, Bernard Miles (d.1991), Kenneth More (d.1982), Robert Morley (d.1992), David Niven (d.1983), Laurence Olivier (d.1989), Cecil Parker (d.1971), Nigel Patrick (d.1981), Dennis Price (d.1973), Anthony Quayle (d.1989), Michael Redgrave (d.1985), Michael Rennie (d.1971), Ralph Richardson (d.1983), James Robertson Justice (d.1975), Paul Scofield (d.2008), Peter Sellers (d.1980), Alistair Sim (d.1976), Donald Sinden, Anthony Steel (d.2001), Terry Thomas (d.1990), Richard Todd, David Tomlinson (d.2000), Bill Travers (d.1994), Jack Warner (d.1981), Michael Wilding (d.1979), and Kenneth Williams (d.1988).

However good and entertaining the British-made films were, it must be acknowledged that American films dominated our cinema screens with countless big-screen classics, and with some films they introduced us to newly developed widescreen technology, such as Cinemascope, Vista Vision and Cinerama, as well as new and improved techniques in the use of 3D colour film.

Epic films from American-owned studios included *The Robe* (1953), *The Ten Commandments* (1956), *The 7th Voyage of Sinbad* (1958) and *Ben-Hur* (1959). Hollywood enabled British-born filmmaker Alfred Hitchcock to make some of the best mystery suspense thrillers ever made. Walt Disney

Productions released dozens of captivating films in the '50s, including *Cinderella* (1950), *Treasure Island* (1950), *Alice in Wonderland* (1951), *Peter Pan* (1953), *Lady and the Tramp* (1955), *Davy Crockett, King of the Wild Frontier* (1955) and *Sleeping Beauty* (1959).

Who could ever forget going to the pictures as a child, and seeing the big red curtains fold back to expose that giant screen that suddenly burst into life with the MGM roaring lion, signalling the start of the film's opening credits? Or, there was Columbia's 'Torch Lady' logo of a lady stood on a pedestal carrying a torch and draped in a flag. All of the big production companies had their own unique, attention-grabbing symbols. You will remember the 20th Century Fox logo with the moving searchlights and dramatic fanfare. But, best of all, was the trademark 'gongman' of the British filmmaking company, the Rank Organisation. The 'man with the gong' was used as an introduction to all J. Arthur Rank films. It was not the most lavishly produced piece of film, but it is probably the best and most fondly remembered, and it was British!

Memorable films made in the USA during the 1950s included: *Singin' in the Rain* (1952), *From Here to Eternity* (1953), *Roman Holiday* (1953), *The Caine Mutiny* (1954), *On the Waterfront* (1954), *Rear Window* (1954), *Seven Brides for Seven Brothers* (1954), *East of Eden* (1955), *Guys and Dolls* (1955), *Rebel Without a Cause* (1955) and *12 Angry Men* (1957). However, you will just as easily recall some of those old 1930s and '40s films that were shown again and again throughout the 1950s: films like the classic gangster film, *Angels with Dirty Faces*, with James Cagney, Pat O'Brien, Humphrey Bogart and the Dead End Kids.

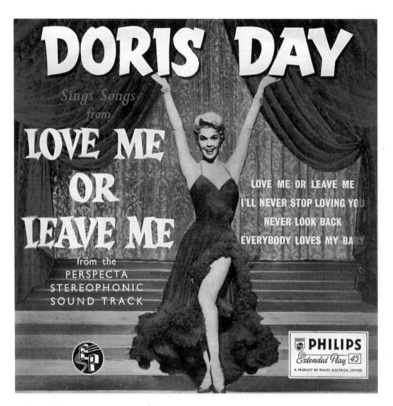

All the kids loved Doris Day after seeing her star in *Calamity Jane*, with all those wonderful songs that you just couldn't get out of your head. She made the film *Love Me or Leave Me* in 1955, and became the first actress to get star billing over James Cagney in thirty years, and he got her the part!

There were so many inspiring stars of American films around in the 1950s, far too numerous to mention. Here are just a few of those that kept the kids on the edge of their seats: Fred Astaire, Lauren Bacall, Ingrid Bergman, Humphrey Bogart, James Cagney, Charles Chaplin, Joan Crawford, Bette Davis, James Dean, Kirk Douglas, Henry Fonda, Cary Grant, Audrey Hepburn, Katherine Hepburn,

William Holden, Gene Kelly, Grace Kelly, Burt Lancaster, Sophia Loren, Robert Mitchum, Marilyn Monroe, Gregory Peck, Edward G. Robinson, Ginger Rogers, James Stewart, Shirley Temple, Spencer Tracey, and the inimitable John Wayne.

Yes, the cinema was great escapism, and everyone's favourite night out – choc-ice, popcorn … oh, and … A-u-r-o-r-a, don't forget the Kia-Ora!

Popular Music

The 1950s are fondly remembered as the decade of 'rock and roll' music, but in reality, the record buyers were suckers for ballads, and, throughout the '50s, home-grown heart-throb ballad singers like Dickie Valentine, Jimmy Young, Ronnie Hilton and Michael Holliday had British girls swooning in the aisles. American artists like Nat 'King' Cole, Bing Crosby, Tony Bennett and Perry Como also managed to retain their popularity in Britain, particularly Perry Como, who had seven top ten hits in the late '50s and, after rock and roll had hit Britain, a number one in 1958 with *Magic Moments.* There were plenty of successful female artists around, like Ruby Murray and Connie Francis, but the 1950s was the age of the male ballad singers and the teen idols.

The big band music that dominated the 1930s and 1940s was much less favoured in the 1950s, but some of the established American big band singers like Frank Sinatra and Doris Day had already crossed over into films, and by the 1950s they were world famous. Singers such as these attracted a whole new set of '50s teenage fans flocking to

Music papers and songbooks weren't just for teenagers. Kids of all ages pawed through them to learn whatever they could about popular artists and their music.

see their films and to buy their records. From 1952 (record charts were first published in November 1952) to 1959, Doris Day had eight top ten records in the British charts, including two number one hits, *Secret Love* in 1954, and *Whatever Will Be Will Be* in 1956. Frank Sinatra had six top ten records during the same period, including his number one hit, *Three Coins in a Fountain* in 1954.

Rock and roll arrived in Britain in December 1954 with Bill Haley and his Comets' *Shake Rattle and Roll*, and Lonnie

Donegan introduced us to skiffle music in 1955 with *Rock Island Line*. These two records added a significant new dimension to popular music, and subsequently influenced a host of British artists to launch pop music careers – artists like Cliff Richard, who had his first hit record in 1958 with *Move It*, which is credited as being the first rock and roll song produced outside the United States. In the late '50s, Cliff Richard and the Drifters (who became the Shadows in 1959) had another four top ten records in the British charts, including two number ones, *Living Doll* and *Travellin' Light*, both in 1959 – the rest is history! Lonnie Donegan, 'King of Skiffle', had eleven top ten hits in the late 1950s, including two number ones in 1957, *Cumberland Gap* and *Gamblin' Man/Putting on the Style*. He also topped the charts in March 1960 with *My Old Man's a Dustman*. Bill Haley and his Comets had nine top ten hits in Britain during the same period, including the number one hit single *Rock Around the Clock* in October 1955. It was the first record ever to sell over one million copies in Britain, but it didn't make the top spot when it was first released in January of that year. It was the film *Blackboard Jungle*, which was released later in the year and featured the song in the opening and closing titles, that sparked renewed interest in *Rock Around the Clock* and made it a number one hit in Britain. Elvis Presley, the 'King of Rock and Roll', was ever present in the UK charts from May 1956 onwards, and he was particularly dominant in 1957–58, but it was Frankie Lane who was the biggest charting artist of the 1950s.

Tommy Steele had six UK top ten hits in the late '50s, including the number one hit single *Singing The Blues* in

1956. Although he started out in 1956 as a rock and roller with his first record *Rock with the Cavemen*, by the end of the '50s his musical style had changed somewhat, as indicated by his 1959 hit single, *Little White Bull*. Marty Wilde had five 'moody teenager style' top ten hits in the late '50s, including a number two record with *Teenager in Love* in 1959, and he reached number three in the charts that same year with *Sea of Love*. Although Billy Fury had a couple of hit records in the '50s with *Maybe Tomorrow* and *Margo*, he didn't achieve top-ten chart success until the 1960s. Likewise, Adam Faith is sometimes thought of as a successful product of the 1950s, but he didn't achieve his first hit single until November 1959 when *What Do You Want* reached number one in the UK charts. Again, his most successful pop music days were in the 1960s.

Other British popular music artists that remained successful throughout the 1950s included: Winifred Atwell, pianist, who had eleven top ten hits, including *Poor People of Paris*, which reached number one in the UK charts in 1956; Shirley Bassey, who had three top ten hits, including *As I Love You* in 1959; Max Bygraves, who had six top ten hits, and a highest chart position of number two with *Meet Me on the Corner* in 1955; Alma Cogan with four top ten hits including the number one hit single *Dreamboat* in 1955; Russ Conway, pianist, who had six top ten hits including two number ones, *Side Saddle* and *Roulette* both in 1959; Ronnie Hilton, who had five top ten hits including one number one, *No Other Love* in 1956; Michael Holliday, who was very popular but only had two top ten hit records, including *The Story of My Life*, which reached number one in 1958, and *Starry Eyed*, which claimed the number one

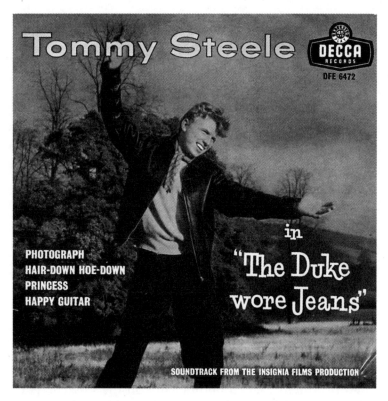

Tommy Steele is widely regarded as Britain's first 'teen idol' and 'rock 'n' roll' star. By 1957, the cheeky Cockney had moved into films and *The Duke Wore Blue Jeans* was his second film of 1957.

spot again in January 1960; Vera Lynn, who had five top ten hits, including *My Son My Son*, which reached number one in 1954; Ruby Murray, who had eight top ten hits, including *Softly, Softly*, which reached number one in 1955; Dickie Valentine who had eight top ten hits, including two number one hits, *Finger of Suspicion* in 1954 and *Christmas Alphabet* in 1955; Frankie Vaughan, who had eight top ten hits, including *Garden of Eden*, which reached number one in 1957; Malcolm Vaughan, who had four top ten hits, but although very popular never reached number one in the charts; David Whitfield, who had eleven top ten hit records, including two number ones, *Answer Me* in 1953 and *Cara Mia* in 1954; Jimmy Young (he of long-time Radio DJ Fame) who had five top ten hits, including two number ones, *Unchained Melody* in 1955 and *The Man From Laramie* in 1955.

Successful American artists included: Paul Anka, who had six top ten hits, including *Diana*, which went to number one in 1957; Tony Bennett, who had only one top ten hit, *Stranger in Paradise*, which went to number one in 1955; Pat Boone, who had ten UK top ten hits in the 1950s, including the number one hit single *I'll Be Home* in 1956; Nat 'King' Cole, who had thirteen top ten hits, but surprisingly no number ones; Bing Crosby, who had six top ten hits, but no number ones; Bobbie Darin, who had two top ten hits, *Dream Lover* and *Mack the Knife*, and they both went to number one in 1959; The Everly Brothers, who had six top ten hits, including *All I Have to Do is Dream/ Claudette*, a double A-side that reached number one in the British charts in 1958, but had to wait until 1960 to get their biggest-selling record and number one hit, *Cathy's Clown*; Connie Francis, who had four top ten hits, including two number ones, *Who's Sorry Now* and *Carolina Moon/Stupid Cupid*, both in 1958; Buddy Holly, who had three top ten hits, including *It Doesn't Matter Any More*, which reached number one in 1959; Frankie Lane, who had nineteen top ten hits (including four duets) and four number ones, *I Believe* in 1953, *Hey Joe* in 1953, *Answer Me* in 1953 and *A Woman In Love* in 1956; Jerry Lee Lewis, who had three top ten hits, including *Great Balls Of Fire*, which reached number one in the British charts in December 1957; Little Richard, who had five top ten hits, but no number ones; Dean Martin, who had nine UK top ten hits in the 1950s, including the number one hit single *Memories are Made of This* in 1956; Al Martino, who had six UK top ten hits in the 1950s, including the number one hit single *Here in My Heart* in 1952; Guy Mitchell, who had thirteen top ten hits including four number ones, *She Wears Red Feathers* in 1953, *Look at that Girl* in 1953, *Singing the Blues* in 1956 and *Rock-a-Billy* in 1957; Ricky Nelson, who had three top ten hits in the late '50s, but no number one hits; Elvis Presley, who had eighteen top ten hits, including four number ones, *All Shook Up* in 1957, *Jailhouse Rock* in 1958, *One Night/I Got Stung* in 1959 and *A Fool Such as I/I Need Your Love Tonight* in 1959; Johnnie Ray, who had ten top ten hits, including three number ones, *Such A Night* in 1954, *Just Walkin' in the Rain* in 1956 and *Yes Tonight Josephine* in 1957; and Kay Starr, who had four top ten hits, including two number ones, *Comes a-Long a-Love* in 1952 and *Rock and Roll Waltz* in 1956.

You will also remember singers like Billy Fury, Bobby Rydell and Bobby Vee from the '50s, but they didn't have hit records in Britain until the early '60s, and although 'rockers' like Chuck Berry were very popular in Britain in the late '50s, he had to wait until 1963 to get into the UK top ten with *Let it Rock/Memphis Tennessee*, a double A-side. Similarly, Fats Domino was very well-liked in Britain and had twelve records enter the top thirty from 1956–59, but his only top ten hit during the '50s was *Blueberry Hill*, which reached number six in the UK charts in 1956.

The first Eurovision Song Contest was in 1956, and Britain's first entry was in 1957 with *All*, sung by Patricia Bredin, which came seventh out of the ten countries that entered. The UK didn't enter the 1958 contest, and to date it is the only year we have not taken part. In 1959, the competition was held in Cannes, and the United Kingdom came second with *Sing Little Birdie*, which was sung by husband and wife duo, Pearl Carr and Teddy Johnson. The song reached number twelve in the UK charts.

As in every decade, novelty records were popular in the 1950s, and you will remember that many were regularly played on Uncle Mac's Children's Favourites show every Saturday morning on BBC radio. You will undoubtedly recall two in particular, *I Tawt I Taw a Puddy Tat* by Mel Blanc, which was number one in the sheet music charts for three weeks in January 1951 (this was before record charts started to be published), and *How Much is that Doggie in the Window* by Lita Roza, which reached number one in the UK hit record charts in April 1953, but for one week only.

Fashion

As in every generation, affluent parents bought their children expensive designer clothes and dressed them in their own fashionable image. Women's magazines were full of fashion ideas for the whole family. There were pictures of young boys dressed in two-piece made-to-measure suits that made them look like a miniature version of their dad; the only difference was that the child's suit had short trousers with turn-ups. Many magazines catered for the proud mums who loved to dress up their little girls in pretty fashionable clothes. The pages were often filled with pictures of young girls dressed in smart, brightly coloured pinafore dresses, pleated skirts, and well-tailored jackets with matching beret-style caps. Lots of puff-sleeve blouses, with plenty of ribbons and bows, and brightly coloured shoes. To the average family, this was all Hollywood stuff and well beyond their means; so, out would come the sewing machine, and your mum would try her hand at making something resembling the real thing. Dressmaking was something that all mums seemed to be able to do, a skill that was taught and handed down through generations. Young girls' dresses in the '50s were usually loose fitting, cut just above the knee, and gathered at the waist with a belt or a ribbon. Mums were also quite adept when it came to copying fashionable hairstyles. It took time, but it cost nothing to send their child out with well-groomed hair. Girls from ordinary working-class families would frequently have their hair smartly styled in ringlets, bunches, plaits or in a ponytail – sometimes with a fringe, and usually held in place with an Alice band or ribbons. And then there were the hair grips that they were forever taking out, pinching apart with their teeth and pushing back in place. Short hair, parted on the left side, was also quite fashionable for young girls. However you were dressed, and for whatever occasion, young girls always wore navy blue knickers, and boys always wore white y-fronts. One item of clothing that was common to both boys and girls was the vest – you always had to wear a white sleeveless vest under your shirt or blouse.

Many 1950s designer fashions for men wouldn't look out of place today: stylish polo shirts (then called a tennis shirt) with brightly coloured horizontal stripes, short-sleeved check-patterned shirts, sports jackets with patch pockets, and well-tailored single or double-breasted suits. On the other hand, the trilby hats and decorative top-pocket hankies thankfully fell by the wayside long ago! Although women's fashions always seem to return if you wait long enough, there has never been a resurgence in the popularity of such '50s things as women's hats, or brightly coloured figure-hugging flared dresses, tied into tiny corseted waists with belts of ribbon and bows.

Although it was only the wealthy that could afford to buy designer clothes and be truly fashionable, many less well-off women tried to be as up to date as possible with clothing trends, mostly by dressmaking and knitting the clothes themselves. Conversely, the ordinary man in the street usually wore sensible and boring clothes. Many frequently dressed in their World War Two demob suit for everyday purposes well into the 1950s. There were lots of hand-knitted woollen cardigans, sleeveless jumpers and socks. Hand-knitted socks! They were so uncomfortable to wear, especially after they had been darned. Men regularly wore a shirt and tie, complete with tie-pin and cufflinks, and their jacket pocket would often be bulging from the tobacco tin that was always close at hand, ready to roll a fresh cigarette or to fill a pipe. Although men's socks were ribbed at the top, they lacked grip and would continually slide down. Some men wore sock suspenders to keep them up.

In wintertime, because the majority of people walked or used the buses, everyone wore calf-length topcoats to protect them from the weather, and many also wore gloves. Women, as always, were very attached to their handbags, and strapless hand-held bags were popular, but they had to be big enough to hold the essential lipstick and powder compact, and, as many women smoked, there had to be room to accommodate their cigarettes and lighter. Lots of women, and men for that matter, transferred their cigarettes into slim cigarette cases, which took up less space and were very fashionable at the time; they also made popular Christmas presents. Cigarette cases were usually made from silver, leather, chrome or Bakelite, and they were often personalised with the owner's initials engraved on a plate at the front. Other women's fashions included ski pants, pencil skirts, mittens, long gloves, headscarves, tiered skirts, balloon or puffed-sleeved blouses, Duffle coats, short fitted jackets, tight-fitting jumpers, upturned collars, stiletto heels (casual shoes were reserved for the garden or beach), slingback shoes and sandals, and winklepicker shoes. The dresses and blouses always had lots of buttons and pleats sewn into them. Short wavy hair, parted on the left and flicked up at the ends, was very fashionable for women, and so hairnet and curlers were often worn in bed at night. Many women had their hair 'set' at the hairdressers as often as they could afford it, and permed (permanent wave) every few months to make the newly grown hair wavy.

Women generally took great pride in their appearance, and although times were hard, they would always dress presentably and ready to go out if they unexpectedly needed to. Lightweight housecoats or full-length aprons were commonly worn to protect good clothes from getting dirty from housework. However, contrary to the image projected in films, men never wore quilted dressing gowns to protect their clothes around the house – maybe they did in Hollywood!

Teddy Boys and Edwardians

Teddy boys, or 'Teds' as they were often called, got their name from the Edwardian-inspired style of clothes they wore. London teenagers started the fashion in the early 1950s, and they quickly linked themselves to the newly arrived American rock and roll music. The Teddy boy culture soon spread across the country, with some forming gangs. They hung around in cafes and on street corners, sometimes causing trouble and involving themselves in violent confrontations with rival gangs. These punch-ups often involved the use of weapons, such as flick-knives, knuckledusters and bottles. They wore long drape jackets with velvet trim collars and large flapped pockets, white shirts with bootlace 'slim-jim' ties, high-waisted drainpipe trousers, brightly coloured socks and chunky suede shoes, preferably large crepe-soled shoes (known as brothel creepers), which best suited their bouncy movements when jiving to rock and roll music. Their hair was long and was greased up with Vaseline or Brylcreem. They styled it using their treasured and ever-present comb, carefully sculpturing the hair into a huge quiff, and sweeping the sides around to the back of the head to form what was know as a DA (duck's arse).

Although they are invariably linked to 1950s violence, the media often exaggerates the amount of violence and the numbers of Teddy boys involved. There were not enough

Teddy boys around for them to affect people's lives too much. They were a bit of a novelty, and when you saw them in the street you couldn't help but stare at them because they were so flamboyantly dressed in otherwise unfussy surroundings. Policemen still walked the beat back then, and they enforced a no-loitering law, which meant that anyone hanging around on a street corner for more than a few minutes would soon be approached by a policeman, questioned, and moved on. Most 'Teds' became Teddy boys for the clothes and the rock and roll music, and the clothes were too expensive for 'Teds' to risk getting them spoiled in fights. The drape jackets were well tailored and frequently made-to-measure, and they cost a fortune! Teddy boys usually paid for their clothes weekly, on the never-never. Their clothes, records, and of course their treasured comb, were their most prized possessions.

Edwardians, or neo-Edwardians as they should be called, also wore drapes but their style was a lot different to that of the Teddy boys. The smart Edwardian style of fashion became popular with young people a couple of years before Teddy boys came along and adopted the look and took it a stage further to make it much more flashy. It was the newspapers in 1953 who first coined the term 'Teddy', from 'Edward', when describing this new teenage style. Neo-Edwardians wore smart long drape jackets, tailormade from good quality material, slim tailored trousers, white shirt, silk tie, waistcoat, and fine quality Italian shoes. Their hair was fairly short, neatly combed and without the Teddy boy quiff. Again, the neo-Edwardians spent so much money on clothes, it was unlikely that they would go out looking for punch-ups!

Six

RADIO AND TELEVISION

Radio

Memories of 1950s radio programmes remain indelibly imprinted on the minds of those who are old enough to remember when radio was the main source of entertainment in the home. Even with the increasing demand for televisions during the late 1950s, radio was still hugely popular and more than adequately bridged the gaps in between the good television programmes, and filled the time when television's two broadcasting stations, BBC and ITV, were off-air. Well-liked radio shows like *The Goons, Hancock's Half Hour, The Archers* and *Mrs Dale's Diary* continued to attract large numbers of listeners to the BBC radio's Home Service and Light Programme, while Radio Luxembourg, *'208 – your station of the stars'*, was attracting younger listeners through its increased output of pop music.

Your parents had control over the radio's tuning knob, and children often had little say in what programmes were listened to, but there were plenty of radio shows like *Dick Barton*, *Life with the Lyons* and *Meet the Huggetts*, that managed to get both young and old equally hooked. Even with the advent of television programmes like *Watch With Mother* and *Children's Hour*, radio shows like *Uncle Mac's Children's Favourite*, *The Clitheroe Kid* and *Educating Archie* still remained firm favourites with young listeners. As a child in the 1950s, you would have considered the radio announcers and commentators to be just old fuddy-duddies, but you heard so much of them during those radio days that many of their names would still be very familiar to you, such names as Franklin Engelmann, Robert Dougall, Jean Metcalfe, Kenneth Kendal, Alvar Lidell and John Snagge, just to mention a few.

Radio provided great entertainment for you on rainy days, evenings and weekends; and not forgetting the great comfort it could be when you were off school sick with one of those many childhood illnesses of the 1950s. The enormous variety of comedy, drama and music programmes kept you from getting bored and in many ways added to your education. Here is just a selection of popular 1950s radio shows to stir the old grey cells:

A Life of Bliss (1953–9) BBC Light Programme. Written by Godfrey Harrison and featured George Cole as the bumbling David Alexander Bliss who was always finding himself in awkward situations. Petula Clark joined the cast in 1957, and played David Bliss's girlfriend Penny Gay, until she left him at the altar! Animal imitator, Percy Edwards, played Psyche the dog.

The Archers (1951–present) BBC Light Programme and BBC Home Service – 'an everyday story of country folk'. First main broadcast was in January 1951. This is the world's longest-running radio soap, now broadcast on BBC's Radio Four. According to the BBC's press office in 2006, it remained BBC Radio 4's most popular non-news programme. In the 1950s, the story revolved around the Archer family of Brookfield farm near the village of Ambridge. Much of the action took place at the farm or in *The Bull* pub in the village. Some of the main early characters were Dan and Doris Archer, Jack and Peggy Archer, Doris and Jack Woolley, Ned Larkin, Tom Forrest, and of course that old favourite – 'well me old pal, me old beauties' – Walter Gabriel.

Who could ever forget the happy-go-lucky 'maypole dance' theme tune entitled *Barwick Green*?

Beyond Our Ken (1958–64) BBC Light Programme (1950s). This comedy show starred Kenneth Horne, Kenneth Williams, Betty Marsden, Hugh Paddick and Bill Pertwee. Barry Took and Eric Merriman wrote the 1950s' scripts and Douglas Smith played the very formal announcer. It reappeared as *Round the Horne* in 1965–8.

The Billy Cotton Bandshow (1949–68) BBC Light Programme (1950s). The dreaded shout of Billy Cotton's 'Wakey! Wakey!' each Sunday afternoon sent a shiver down every child's spine. This music and comedy show presented by the larger-than-life bandleader, Billy Cotton, also featured Alan Breeze, Doreen Stephens and Kathie Kay. Its lifespan indicates that it was very popular with listeners, but I am not sure that there was ever a poll done of children's views.

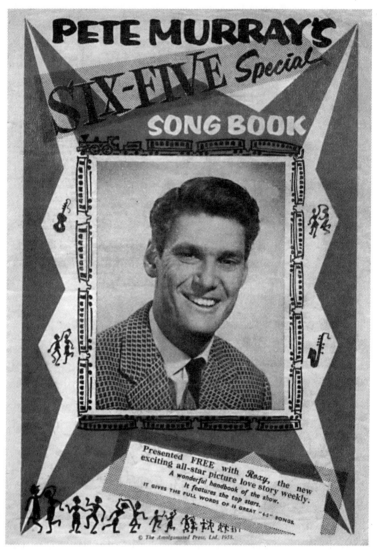

Pete Murray presented *Six-Five Special* live music show on BBC TV in 1957/8, and in 1958 he lent his name to this songbook, which gave the words of sixteen current songs. The songbook came free with Roxy, 'the new exciting all-star picture love story weekly'.

Children's Favourites (1954–67) BBC Light Programme (1950s). Every Saturday morning, Derek McCulloch (Uncle Mac) would play a selection of children's record requests, starting each programme with the words, 'Hello children, everywhere!' Among the most popular record requests from children were *The Laughing Policeman* by Charles Penrose, *Buttons and Bows* by Dinah Shore, *The Runaway Train* by Michael Holliday, *When You Come to the End of a Lollipop* by Max Bygraves, *Nellie the Elephant* by Mandy Miller, *I Tawt I Taw a Puddy Tat* by Mel Blanc, *The Bee Song* by Arthur Askey, *How Much is that Doggy in the Window* by Lita Roza, *The Ugly Duckling* by Danny Kaye, *The Hippopotamus Song* by Flanders and Swann, *Little White Duck* by Danny Kaye, *The Deadwood Stage* by Doris Day, *My Old Man's a Dustman* by Lonnie Donegan, *The Teddy Bear's Picnic* by Henry Hall, *Puff the Magic Dragon* by Peter Paul and *Mary, Que Será Será* by Doris Day. There were just too many regular children's favourites to mention them all. Most children just wrote to the show in the hope of getting their name read out on the radio by Uncle Mac, thereby obtaining full bragging rights in the playground on the following Monday morning!

Children's Hour (1922–64) BBC Home Service (1950s). Broadcast from 5pm to 6pm on weekdays. It was filled with stories, plays and drama serials, as well as informative talks, children's newsreels and competitions. The various presenters included Derek McCulloch, 'Uncle' Arthur Burrows, 'Auntie' Violet Carson, Jon Pertwee and Wilfred Pickles. Popular serials included *Jennings at School, Just So Stories for Little Children, Sherlock Holmes, Worzel Gummidge* and *Winnie the Pooh.*

The Clitheroe Kid (1957–72) BBC Light Programme (1950s). This was a long-running situation comedy programme, featuring the diminutive Northern comedian, Jimmy Clitheroe, who played the part of a cheeky schoolboy. Amazingly, Jimmy Clitheroe was already an experienced thirty-five-year-old comedy actor when *The Clitheroe Kid* was first launched on radio in 1957. Famous celebrities that appeared in the 1950s' programmes included Judith Chalmers, Bob Monkhouse and Violet Carson (best known for her role as Ena Sharples in *Coronation Street*).

Desert Island Discs (1942–present) BBC Home Service (1950s). This programme was devised and presented by Roy Plomley from 1942 until his death in 1985. Each week, a guest was invited to choose eight gramophone records and one book. It is said to be the longest-running music radio show in radio history. It was not essential listening for 1950s kids as most of the musical choices seemed to be either classical or from stage shows. The signature tune was, and still is, *By the Sleepy Lagoon* by Eric Coates.

Dick Barton, Special Agent (1946–51) BBC Light Programme. This was the BBC radio's first daily serial. Our special agent hero, former Commando Captain Richard Barton, with his two trusty sidekicks, Jock Anderson and Snowy White, solved endless crimes and regularly saved us all from terrible disasters. Its unforgettably dramatic chase signature tune was *Devil's Gallop*, composed by Charles Williams.

Easy Beat (1959–67) BBC Light Programme. A Sunday mid-morning show produced and presented by Brian Matthew, it was recorded before a live audience at the Playhouse Theatre, just off Trafalgar Square in London. It featured the Johnny Howard Band, with guest bands and artists including regulars like Kenny Ball's Jazzmen and Bert Weedon.

Educating Archie (1950–60) BBC Light Programme and Home Service. Yes, ventriloquist Peter Brough really did manage to succeed with his own Sunday lunchtime comedy radio show, which he did while holding his dummy, Archie Andrews, in front of the microphone. The show featured fourteen-year-old Julie Andrews, and an enormous number of comedians who went on to become big names, including Tony Hancock, Max Bygraves, Harry Secombe, Benny Hill, Beryl Reid, Hattie Jacques, Dick Emery, Bruce Forsyth, Sid James, Marty Feldman, Graham Stark, Warren Mitchell and James Robertson Justice. The show was even adapted for an ITV television series in 1958.

The Goon Show (1952–60) BBC Home Service with repeats on the BBC Light Programme. Created and mainly written by Spike Milligan, this comedy sketch show was a firm favourite with 1950s kids, including Prince Charles. The show stared Spike Milligan, Harry Secombe, Peter Sellers, and Michael Bentine, who left the show in 1953. Some of the main characters were: Mr Henry Crun, Lance Brigadier Grytpype-Thynne, Major Dennis Bloodnok and Bluebottle – all played by Peter Sellers; Miss Minnie Bannister, Eccles and Moriarty – all played by Spike Milligan; and Ned Seagoon – played by Harry Secombe. Each of the cast played many minor characters as well, and everything was accompanied by music and comical sound affects.

Hancock's Half Hour (1954–9) BBC Light Programme. Comedy show written by Ray Galton and Alan Simpson about the life of down-at-heel comedian, Anthony Aloysius St John Hancock, who was waiting for the big time to arrive. The main character, Hancock, lived with his dim-witted Australian lodger, played by Bill Kerr, at 23 Railway Cuttings, East Cheam. Sid James played Hancock's roguish friend Sid, and in later series, Hattie Jacques played his live-in secretary, Miss Griselda Pugh.

Have A Go (1946–67) BBC Light Programme. A travelling radio quiz, hosted by Yorkshireman Wilfred Pickles, the first BBC newsreader to speak with a broad Yorkshire accent. Accompanied by his wife Mabel, Wilfred took the programme to church halls all around the country, challenging ordinary people to 'have a go' and answer quiz questions for money prizes. With 'Mabel at the table', Wilfred coined several catchphrases, including 'How do, how are yer?', 'Are yer courting?' to the younger contestants, and 'Give 'em the money, Mabel!' when they won, but all contestants were given the money anyway. The theme tune was *Have a Go, Joe* by Jack Jordan, the original pianist on the show. Violet Carson, famous for playing Ena Sharpes in *Coronation Street*, took over as pianist from 1947 to 1953, after that Harry Hudson took over, followed by Eric James in 1966.

Housewives' Choice (1946–67) BBC Light Programme. A popular record request programme for women at home during the day. It was mainly men that presented the shows, with the most popular presenter probably being George Elrick, known as 'The Smiling Face of Radio'; he had a long association with the show. The signature tune was *In Party Mood* by Jack Strachey, another unforgettable tune from the 1950s!

Journey into Space (1953–8) BBC Light Programme. This 1950s radio science fiction classic kept us all up late and sent us to bed with nightmares! Written and produced by BBC producer Charles Chilton, it was set in the future of 1965 and described Man's conquest of the moon. Each half-hour weekly episode left us all biting our fingernails in suspense with a new cliffhanger ending. The main characters included Captain Andrew 'Jet' Morgan, Doc Matthews, Stephen 'Mitch' Mitchell, and Lemuel 'Lemmey' Barnett, with a changing cast that included Andrew Faulds, David Jacobs, David Kossoff and Alfie Bass.

Life with the Lyons (1950–61) BBC Light Programme. A popular light-hearted domestic radio sitcom that featured a real-life American family living in London, and starred the husband and wife team of Ben Lyon and Bebe Daniels, with their children Richard and Barbara Lyon, and the family's pet dog Skeeter. Other cast members included Molly Weir, who played their Scottish housekeeper Aggie McDonald, Doris Rogers, who played the nosey neighbour Florrie Wainwright, and Ian Sadler as her hen-pecked husband George.

Listen with Mother (1950–82) BBC Light Programme (1950s). A fifteen-minute programme of stories, songs and nursery rhymes, it was broadcast every weekday afternoon at 1.45pm for very young children and their mothers. 'Are you sitting comfortably? Then I'll begin!' Presenters and story readers included Daphne Oxenford, Dorothy Smith and Julia Lang.

Meet The Huggetts (1953–61) BBC Light Programme. Comedy series about a London East End charwoman and her family, starring Kathleen Harrison as Ethel, and Jack Warner as Joe.

Mrs Dale's Diary (1948–69) BBC Light Programme (1950s). This was the first post-war daily weekday soap on British radio. It centred on the fictional life of Mrs (Mary) Dale, the wife of a doctor (Jim), and her family life at Virginia Lodge in the fictional London suburb of Parkwood Hill in Middlesex. Ellis Powell played Mrs Dale up until 1963, when Jessie Matthews replaced her. This was essential comfort listening for kids off school sick.

Much-Binding-in-the-Marsh (1944–54) BBC Light Programme; Radio Luxembourg also produced a series of the show in 1950–1. A comedy series about the goings-on at a fictional RAF station, which, after the war, evolved into a newspaper, *The Weekly Bind*. The show was written by and starred Kenneth Horne and Richard 'Stinker' Murdoch; other cast members included Sam Costa, Maurice Denham, Dora Bryan and Nicholas Parsons.

Music While You Work (1940–67) BBC Light Programme (1950s). This was a half-hour show that featured a different live band or orchestra each weekday morning and afternoon, playing a non-stop medley of popular tunes. Its signature tune was *Calling All Workers* by Eric Coates.

Paul Temple (1938–68) BBC Light Programme (1950s). Based on the novels by Francis Durbridge, this fictional amateur detective, with the assistance of his wife Steve, solved all sorts of crime mysteries. Several actors and actresses have portrayed the Temples over the years, with the best-known 1950s stars being Peter Coke and Marjorie Westbury. This was another great mystery serial that had children of the time captivated. The theme music, inspired by the rhythm of a train journey, was *Coronation Scot* by Vivian Ellis.

Pick of the Pops (1955–72) BBC Light Programme (1950s). First presented by forty-seven-year-old Franklin Englemann in 1955, it featured 'newly released gramophone records'. Alan Dell, a more suitable thirty-two-year-old, took over in 1956, playing 'a selection of the latest popular gramophone records'. David Jacobs, then a thirty-year-old, took temporary charge in September 1956 before taking over completely in 1958, when it was moved from mid-week to a Saturday night slot and records were first played from a BBC devised Pop Chart. The show's best-known presenter, Alan 'Fluff' Freeman, made his first appearance on the show in 1961. The signature tune was *At the Sign of the Swinging Cymbal* by Brian Fahey and his Orchestra.

Record Round Up (1948–68) BBC Light Programme (1950s). Jack Jackson, former bandleader turned disc-jockey, created this unusual pop record show where he interrupted pop records with excerpts from comedy monologues by comedians like Shelley Berman and Bob Newhart. His programme was the first fast-moving zany pop show on British radio, and was said to have inspired later presenters like Kenny Everett.

Saturday Club (1958–69) BBC Light Programme (1950s). Renamed from the *Saturday Skiffle Club*, which had started in June 1957, this live pop music show was presented by Brian Matthew between 10am and noon every Saturday morning and was essential listening for kids of all ages – that is, if you weren't at Saturday Morning Pictures! The show included interviews with guest artists and pre-recorded live performances, as well as record requests and new releases. The programme followed on immediately after *Children's Favourites*, which meant that lots of young kids also got hooked on the show. Many home-grown pop stars of the day appeared, including Cliff Richard, Adam Faith, Marty Wilde and Johnny Kidd, as well as a host of American artists, like the Everly Brothers, Jerry Lee Lewis and Bo Diddley. The cheery welcome of Brian Matthews' 'Hello my ol' mateys!' was a familiar greeting that could be heard in every hairdressers and barbershop throughout the country each Saturday morning, with hairdressers everywhere reaching to fine-tune their radios for crystal clear reception. The theme tune was Humphrey Littleton's *Saturday Jump*.

The Adventures of P.C.49 (1947–53) BBC Light Programme. This light comedy and sleuthing drama series, about an ordinary London Bobby on the beat, was created for radio by Alan Shranks, and featured Brian Reece as the upper-crust Police Constable Archibald Berkeley-Willoughby, solving crimes that were beyond the ability of his superiors. It also starred Joy Shelton as 49's girlfriend Joan Carr, Leslie Perrins as Detective Inspector Wilson, and Eric Phillips as Detective Sergeant Wright. The signature tune was *Changing Moods* by Ronald Hanmer.

The Navy Lark (1959–77) BBC Light Programme (1950s). One of the longest-running comedy radio shows ever. It was a send-up of the Senior Service (the Royal Navy – oldest of the British armed forces), and was about life aboard a fictional Royal Navy frigate called HMS *Troutbridge*. The 1950s cast included: Dennis Price as Lieutenant Price (Number One) in series one; Stephen Murray as Lieutenant Murray (Number One) for series two onwards; Leslie Phillips as Sub Lieutenant Phillips; Jon Pertwee as Chief Petty Officer Pertwee and other characters; Richard Caldicott as Commander Povey; Heather Chasen as Wren

Chasen and other characters; Ronnie Barker as Un-Able Seaman 'Fatso' Johnson and other characters; and Tenniel Evans as Able Seaman Taffy Goldstein and other characters. Laurie Wyman devised the series, and Tommy Reilly and James Moody composed the signature tune, *Trade Wind Hornpipe*. This show was thirty minutes of essential comedy listening every Sunday. 'Left hand down a bit!'

Today (1957–present) BBC Home Service (1950s). An early morning news and current affairs programme first presented by Alan Skempton, who was replaced in 1958 by its long-term and best-known presenter, Jack de Manio, who continued to present the show until 1971. Many will remember listening to the dulcet tones of the hugely popular Jack de Manio, and later his roaming London reporter Monty Modlin, as you dipped your neatly cut bread soldiers into a boiled egg. You would, no doubt, have been late for school if you relied on Jack de Manio's time-checks in the morning. He was notoriously gaffe-prone and often got the time wrong.

Ray's a Laugh (1949–61) BBC Light Programme. A domestic comedy created by and starring comedian Ted Ray, with Kitty Bluett playing his wife and Fred Yule playing his brother-in-law. Other well-known names that regularly appeared were Peter Sellers, Patricia Hayes, Kenneth Connor, Pat Coombs and Graham Stark.

Semprini Serenade (1957–82) BBC Light Programme (1950s). This was another 'easy listening' weekday evening show that would send the kids running for cover. 'Old ones, new ones, loved ones, neglected ones' – Alberto Sempini played them all on keyboard and piano, accompanied by Harry Rabinowitz and the BBC Revue Orchestra.

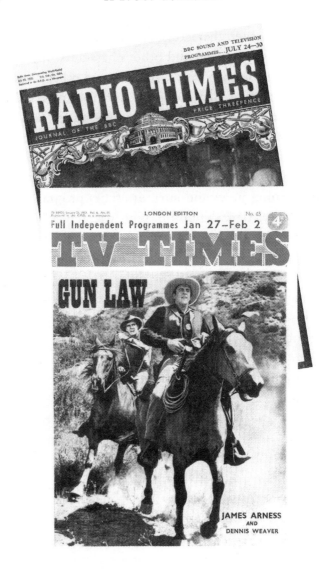

The *Radio Times* gave full radio and television programme listings, and the *TV Times* provided all the information about ITV programmes (often called 'Channel 9'). ITV's *Gun Law* (also produced under the titles of *Gun Smoke* and *Marshal Dillon*) was very popular in the mid to late-1950s. Remember Dennis Weaver who played Chester 'Mis-ter Dil-lon' Goode?

Sing Something Simple (1959–2001) BBC Light Programme (1950s). A torturous half-hour for any child forced to listen to this every Sunday evening, but its longevity proved that it must have been popular with older people. The show featured the Cliff Adams Singers performing a collection of non-stop familiar songs, accompanied by accordionist Jack Emblow and his quartet.

Take It From Here (1948–58) BBC Light Programme. A music and comedy sketch show written by Frank Muir and Denis Norden, and starred Jimmy Edwards, Dick Bentley, Joy Nichols (left in 1953), June Whitfield and Alma Cogan. The show is best remembered for introducing us, in the early 1950s, to a dysfunctional family called The Glums. Jimmy Edwards played Mr Glum, Dick Bentley played his dim-witted son Ron Glum, and June Whitfield played Ron's long-suffering girlfriend Eth. Everyone remembers Eth's regular catchphrase, 'Oh, Ron...!', and Ron's reply, 'Yes, Eth?' The writers filled the show with sharp comedy lines, like this one from the overbearing Mr Glum: 'Ron, run upstairs and fetch me your mother's toothbrush. I've got my new suede shoes on and I've trodden in something.' Kids didn't always understand the TIFH jokes, but The Glums' sketches had everyone in stitches.

Top of the Form (1948–86) BBC Light Programme (1950s). This was radio's general knowledge quiz show for teams of children from secondary schools around the country. However, it mainly featured pupils from grammar and independent schools. The main presenters (question masters) in the 1950s were Kenneth Horne, John Ellison and Robert MacDermott. The quiz involved teams of different age groups and the show was very popular with young listeners, eager to pit their wits against kids of their own age. The rousing theme music was taken from *Marching Strings* by Marshall Ross (a pseudonym of orchestra leader and composer, Ray Martin).

Woman's Hour (1946–present) BBC Light Programme (1950s). A weekday woman's magazine programme that was on between 2pm and 3pm each afternoon. Norman Collins created the programme as a daily line-up of music, advice and entertainment for the home. Jean Metcalfe was its presenter from 1950 to 1958, and then Marjorie Anderson took over until she retired in 1972. This was essential listening for mums at home all day, and another interesting radio show for kids off school with childhood illnesses, particularly boys who would be fascinated by live on-air discussions about women's menstrual problems and the menopause! Yes, they discussed such things on the radio as far back as 1947!

Worker's Playtime (1941–64) Originally on the BBC Home Service then moved to the Light Programme in 1957, until 1964. This was a radio variety touring show that was broadcast live, three days a week, from different factory canteens around the country, as selected by the Ministry of Labour. The programme was produced by Bill Gates and featured countless well-known entertainers, like Charlie Chester, Peter Sellers, Tony Hancock, Frankie Howerd, Anne Sheldon, Betty Driver (now famous for her role as *Coronation Street*'s barmaid, Betty Williams), Eve Boswell, Dorothy Squires, Arthur English, Julie Andrews, Morecambe and Wise, Bob Monkhouse, Ken Dodd, Ken 'I won't take me coat off – I'm not stopping!' Platt, Gert and Daisy (Elsie and Doris Waters) and the impressionist, Peter

Goodwright. Children who listened to the show imagined that working in a factory was fun and was all about having a good time – what was so hard in that?

Radio Luxembourg (1933–92), 208 metres on the medium-wave band. One of the earliest commercial radio stations broadcasting to Britain; it helped pioneer modern radio presentation styles and kick-started the careers of many well-known radio and television celebrities. In the 1950s, it brought back to air a new version of the sponsored Ovaltiney's Concert Party, featuring the *We Are The Ovaltineys* theme song, which Radio Luxembourg first introduced in the early 1930s. In the '50s, you will have stayed up late to listen to Pete Murray present the *Top Twenty* show, one of the earliest pop music shows transmitted on British radio. Up until the 1960s, when the station became predominantly a pop music station, Radio Luxembourg broadcast a wide variety of programmes, including comedy, drama, music and quiz shows. You might well remember listening to such diverse programmes as *The Adventures of Dan Dare, Perry Mason, The Story of Dr Kildare, Take Your Pick* with Michael Miles, and *Double Your Money* with Hughie Green. There were also sports programmes and a host of sponsored religious programmes. Some of the 1950s disc-jockeys and presenters that you may remember included Teddy Johnson (half of the famous Pearl Carr and Teddy Johnson husband-and-wife singing duo), Warren Mitchell, Pete Murray, Barry Alldis, Sam Costa, Alan Dell, Dick Emery (the comedian), Keith Fordyce, Alan 'Fluff' Freeman, David Gell, Tony Hall, Jack Jackson, David Jacobs, Brian Matthew, Don Moss, Ray Orchard, Jimmy Savile, Shaw Taylor, Jimmy Young and Muriel Young. One memory that is surely burned into everyone's mind is that of the Horace Batchelor's 'spot commercials', for the secret to his 'Famous Infra-Draw Method' of winning the football pools – 'and remember, that's Keynsham, spelt K-E-Y-N-S-H-A-M, Bristol'.

Television

It was the day that all of your dreams came true: the day that television came into your home for the first time. That tiny television screen with its 405 lines of grainy black and white picture was just wonderful. This newly acquired entertainment novelty had the whole family hypnotised into watching anything that appeared on the screen – even the BBC's black, grey and white test card that often bridged the gap between transmissions! It's likely that you had already seen some of the programmes on a lucky few friends' and neighbours' television sets, but to have your very own television was another one of those life-changing experiences that made you pinch yourself to believe it was true. Some of your favourite programmes had been previously on the radio, but now you could actually see the stars of those shows in the flesh – or at least in the form of a wishy-washy grey miniature moving picture. So what if your dad did have to keep moving around the room with the aerial to improve reception of the television signal. The furniture in the room was all reorganised to face the television, and the hitherto indispensable radio set was forever consigned to some lonely spot in the room – or was it?

Here is a selection of popular 1950s television shows that will surely bring back some fond memories:

77 Sunset Strip (1958–64) ITV. This was an American private detective series that starred Efrem Zimbalist Jr as Stu' Bailey, and Roger Smith as Jeff Spencer, both former government secret agents. Edd Byrnes played the wisecracking, hair-combing, seriously cool, valet parking attendant from next door, Gerald Lloyd Kookson III, known to all as 'Kookie', the wannabe investigator. The two private detectives worked out of offices at 77 Sunset Strip, next door to Dean Martin's real-life nightclub, *Dino's*. All the girls loved 'Kookie', and his frequent use of the comb led to a huge increase in comb sales in Britain. In 1959, Edd Byrnes teamed up with Connie Stevens to release a pop record called *Kookie, Kookie (Lend Me Your Comb)*, and it reached number twenty-seven in the UK music charts.

Andy Pandy (1950–9) BBC TV. Television's answer to *Listen With Mother*, aimed at toddlers. Andy Pandy was a string puppet portrayed as a three-year-old boy that supposedly acted just like the toddler viewers. The programme included songs and games with Andy Pandy and his friends, Teddy and Looby Loo the rag doll.

The Army Game (1957–61) ITV. Comedy drama series about a group of soldiers doing peacetime National Service in the British Army. The conscripts were determined to do as little work as possible, and lots of comedy capers went on behind the back of the fierce Sergeant Major. The cast included many actors that went on to become household names, including Alfie Bass, Bernard Bresslaw, Dick Emery, Harry Fowler, Bill Frazer, William Hartnell, Charles

Hawtrey, Michael Medwin, Geoffrey Palmer, Norman Rossington and Frank Williams.

The Arthur Haynes Show (1956–66) ITV. A British comedy sketch series starring the talented Arthur Hayes, who was known for his famous portrayal of a tramp ('Up to me neck in muck and bullets!'), a character that was created by Johnny Speight. Other regulars on the show included Nicholas Parsons, Patricia Hayes, Graham Stark and Dermot Kelly who played another tramp called *Irish*. The series only ended because of Arthur Haynes' sudden death in 1966.

Before Your Very Eyes (1956–8) BBC TV and then ITV. Arthur Askey's comedy sketch show, which also featured Anthea Askey (Arthur's daughter), Sabrina (Norma Sykes) and June Whitfield. Sabrina played the dumb blond with a curvaceous figure, and Arthur Askey made endless jokes about her physique. Not one of the most entertaining shows for youngsters, but the talented June Whitfield was always worth a look.

Billy Bunter of Greyfriars School (1952–61) BBC TV. This comedy TV series was based on the fictional books by Frank Richards (real name Charles Hamilton), who also scripted the series. It starred Gerald Campion, who was thirty-nine years old by the time the series ended, as the fat jam-tart and doughnut-loving schoolboy, Billy Bunter. Light-hearted, posh public schoolboy banter and comic bullying, with plenty of 'Oh Crikey!' and 'I say, you fellows!' This series was popular with both children and adults alike, with some episodes being shown twice a day to capture young and old viewers. Future stars that appeared included Anthony Valentine, Ron Moody, Michael Crawford, David

Hemmings and Melvyn Hayes. The theme tune was taken from *Sea Songs* by Vaughan Williams.

The Black and White Minstrel Show (1958–78) BBC TV. This weekly light entertainment and variety show featured The Mitchell Minstrels as 'blacked-up' white performers singing Dixie and Country and Western songs. It was hugely popular with the old folk but it ruined many a child's Saturday night.

Blue Peter (1958–present) BBC TV. Nobody ever thought that *Blue Peter* would evolve into the programme it has become today, or that it would still be running over fifty years down the line. It was first aired on 16 October 1958, and then appeared as a weekly fifteen-minute programme that was aimed at five- to eight-year-olds. The first two presenters were Christopher Trace and Leila Williams, winner of Miss Great Britain in 1957. In the programme, Christopher Trace would demonstrate boys' toys, such as model railways, aeroplanes and trains, and Leila Williams would show girls' toys, mainly dolls, and girls' hobbies. Occasionally, the artist Tony Hart would appear on the programme, using his drawings to tell children's stories. There were no *Blue Peter* badges, pets or ships, and no *Blue Peter* garden. The theme tune was a sea shanty called *Barnacle Bill*. In the 1960s, the programme's running time was extended to twenty-five minutes and it was shown twice a week. In 1962, Leila Williams was removed from the programme by its newly appointed producer. Christopher Trace continued as a *Blue Peter* presenter until 1967.

The Buccaneers (1956–7) ITV. Adventure series which starred Robert Shaw as Dan Tempest, the ex-pirate captain of the *Sultana* gunship. Captain Dan Tempest and his crew of ex-pirates went on a series of swashbuckling high-seas adventures; they were perfectly behaved, with no gambling, stealing or wenching! Children of all ages loved this.

Captain Pugwash (1957–8) BBC TV. Animated television series of short five-minute-long films about the adventures of a fictional pirate called Captain Horatio Pugwash, and his cabin boy called Tom. Captain Pugwash sailed the seven seas with his pirate crew on his ship the *Black Pig*, often encountering the black-bearded villain, Cut-Throat Jake, captain of *The Flying Dustman*.

Cool for Cats (1956–61) ITV. A weekly fifteen-minute pop music show in which presenter Kent Walton played records and reviewed them. The Dougie Squires Dancers, including the then teenager Una Stubbs, performed dance routines to some of the music.

Crackerjack! (1955–84) BBC TV. A weekly children's comedy/variety show. 'It's Friday, it's five to five … It's *Crackerjack!*' Filmed in front of an audience of excited children, this was one of the most popular children's television programmes ever. The show's first presenter was Eamonn Andrews (1955–64), who mimed during the singing, and regular performers included Ronnie Corbett, Joe Baker and Jack Douglas. You would definitely have run home from school to see this. It had everything you needed to help you forget a hard week at school: corny jokes, singalongs, pop star guests, games, quizzes, comedy sketches, and 'Double or Drop', the game where kids' arms were loaded up with prizes as they answered each question correctly, or with cabbages if they got them wrong. They were out of the game if they dropped anything or if they got two questions wrong. Everyone that took part got a Crackerjack pencil, and it was an unwritten rule that whenever the presenter said 'Crackerjack', the audience would shout back loudly, 'Crack-er-jack!'

Criss Cross Quiz (1957–67) ITV. A general knowledge quiz game version of 'Noughts and Crosses'. Jeremy Hawke presented the show in the 1950s.

Dixon of Dock Green (1956–76) BBC TV. Drama series featuring PC George Dixon, played by Jack Warner, who was an old-style London beat-Bobby; solving crime using the soft touch, 'a nice cup of tea and a chat', with the odd 'clip around the ear' for the young tearaways. Jack Warner was sixty years old when the television series first started, but with all the success he had at solving crime, it still took until he was well past retirement age before he got promoted to the rank of sergeant. This was something that mystified even the youngest of minds! 'Evenin' all!'

Double Your Money (1955–68) Rediffusion/ITV. This was a quiz show in which members of the public won cash prizes for answering increasingly difficult general knowledge questions, with the prize money doubling after each answered question. When the prize money reached £32 then contestants had to answer questions from inside a soundproofed sealed glass booth. Hughie Green was the host for the entire life of the show.

Educating Archie (1958–9) ITV. Comedy show similar to that already running on BBC radio. It ran for twenty-seven half-hour episodes on television, and starred Archie Andrews, a ventriloquist's dummy dressed in a broad striped blazer and scarf, with ventriloquist Peter Brough. It also starred Irene Handle as the housekeeper Mrs Twissle, and Dick Emery as Mr Monty. The show was popular with the 250,000 members of the Archie Andrews children's fan club, that had been built up from avid listeners to the radio shows. The trouble with the TV show was that you could see Brough's lips moving – a bit of a problem for a ventriloquist!

Emergency Ward 10 (1957–67) ITV. One of British TV's first soap operas, and the first hospital-based drama. It was about life behind the swing-doors of fictional Oxbridge General Hospital. Its stars included Jill Browne as Nurse Carole Young, Rosemary Miller as Nurse Pat Roberts, Elizabeth Kentish as Sister Cowley and Charles Tingwell as House Surgeon Alan Dawson.

Grandstand (1958–2007) BBC TV. The first programme on British television to pull together a variety of sports into one show. Its first presenter was Peter Dimmock, but David Coleman took over the hot seat just a few weeks later, and he continued to present the show until 1968 when Frank Bough took over.

The Flowerpot Men (1952–4) BBC TV. Part of the *Watch With Mother* series, created and written by Freda Lingstrom. It was about the adventures of a pair of stringed puppets called Bill and Ben, made from small flowerpots that lived side-by-side in two giant flowerpots at the end of the garden, and their friend Little W-e-e-d. The Flowerpot Men would pop out for their adventures when the gardener went for his lunch. They spoke in a strange language of 'flibodobs' and 'flibadobs', while Weed warned them of any danger using her high-pitched voice to say 'Weeeeeed'. There was usually a mishap while they were out of their pots, but who did it? Only the viewers and W-e-e-d knew they were there. 'Was it Bill or was it Ben?'

Hancock's Half Hour (1956–69) BBC TV. This was the television version of the popular radio comedy series. As with the radio shows it starred Tony Hancock as Anthony Aloysius St John Hancock, who continually failed in his attempts to rise above his humble origins. Sid James was the only other cast member to transfer across from radio, although Kenneth Williams and Hattie Jacques made some guest appearances. Liz Frazer, Irene Handl, Hugh Lloyd, John Le Mesurier, Warren Mitchell, Arthur Mullard and Richard Wattis made other guest appearances. Wally Scott composed the distinctive tuba-based theme.

Highway Patrol (1956–8) ITV. This popular American crime/drama cop series made *Dixon of Dock Green* look pretty tame. It starred Broderick Crawford as the fast-talking gravel-voiced Highway Patrol Chief, Dan Matthews, solving crime somewhere in California, with lots of police patrol cars, motorbikes and helicopters chasing down the criminals. Dan Matthews often led the investigations from a patrol car and was known for his police-car-radio catchphrases: 'Ten-Twenty' (report your position), and the one that all the kids mimicked, 'Ten-Four' (message received and understood).

I Love Lucy (1955–65) ITV. One of the first ever family sitcoms shown on ITV when the new channel started in 1955. It starred Lucille Ball as Lucy Ricardo, the scatty wife of singer/bandleader Ricky Ricardo, played by Lucy's real-life husband, Desi Arnaz. In the series, Lucy gets herself into all sorts of madcap situations with friends and landlords Ethel Mertz, played by Vivian Vance, and Fred Mertz, played by William Frawley. This was one of the funniest shows on television in the '50s. Kids and grown-ups loved it!

Ivanhoe (1958–9) ITV. This adventure series starred Roger Moore, in his first leading television role, as Sir Wilfred of Ivanhoe, a medieval knight on a white charger, complete with shiny armour, chainmail and plumed helmet. The heroic knight fought many swashbuckling battles with the wicked Prince John's men, and had never a hair out of place on his neatly quiffed brylcreemed head. All the kids loved it!

Juke Box Jury (1959–67) BBC TV. A pop music panel show in which the host, DJ David Jacobs, played excerpts from the latest pop records and the four-panel celebrity jury made comments and voted the record a 'hit' or a 'miss'. The panel in the early shows featured Alma Cogan (then twenty-seven), Gary Miller (then thirty-five), Pete Murray (then thirty-three), and Susan Stranks (then nineteen). In later series the panel was changed from week to week. The original theme was *Juke Box Fury*, written and performed by Tony Osborne under the name of Ozzie Warlock and the Wizards, but the theme was changed in 1960 to the more familiar *Hit and Miss* by the John Barry Seven.

The Larkins (1958–60) ITV. Comedy situation drama about a family living in the London suburbs and their next-door neighbours, the Prouts. The cast included David Kossoff as Alf Larkins, Peggy Mount as Ada Larkins, Shaun O'Riordon as Eddie Larkins, Ronan O'Casey as Jeff Rogers, Ruth Trouncer as Joyce Rogers, Hilary Bamberger as Myrtle Prout, Barbara Mitchell as Hetty Prout, and George Roderick as Sam Prout.

The Lenny the Lion Show (1957–60) BBC TV. Lenny the lion was a ventriloquist's animal-puppet dummy, and Terry Hall was the ventriloquist. Lenny played a bashful lion with a lisp, unable to pronounce his Rs. He would regularly raise his paw across his head with embarrassment and say his catchphrase 'Aw, don't embawass me!'

Mr Pastry (1950–62) BBC TV. Richard Hearne had been playing Mr Pastry, a comical old man with a walrus moustache in a black suit or raincoat and bowler hat, since 1936. The doddery old Mr Pastry got up to lots of slapstick adventures. In 1958, Richard Hearne started to make a comedy series for ITV called *The Adventures of Mr Pastry* with Buster Keaton, but Buster Keaton became ill and returned to America. The one and only episode that was made of this series was shown on ITV on 21 June 1958. You will also remember Mr Pastry films being shown at Saturday Morning Pictures.

Muffin The Mule (1952–5) BBC TV, and then repeats appeared on ITV during 1956–7. A series of fifteen-minute puppet shows featuring Muffin the mule, with its television creator, Annette Mills (older sister of John Mills), at the piano.

Noddy (*The Adventures of Noddy*) (1955–6) ITV. The adventures of Enid Blyton's 'little nodding man' and his many puppet friends, including Big-Ears, Mr Plod and Bumpy Dog.

Oh Boy! (1958–9) ITV. Rock and roll live music show, produced by Jack Good and presented by Jimmy Henney and Tony Hall. It may have only been on the smallest of silver screens with rubbish sound quality, but it was a very entertaining and exciting show for kids of all ages. The show included live performances by British artists like Cliff Richard, Marty Wilde and Billy Fury, as well as top American artists like The Inkspots, Conway Twitty and Brenda Lee.

Lord Rockingham's Xl were the house band, supported by The Vernon Girls, the Dallas Boys and Neville Taylor's Cutters. Other heart-throbs of the day that also appeared included Ronnie Carroll, The Drifters (later changed their name to The Shadows to avoid confusion with the successful American group called The Drifters), Tommy Steele, the John Barry Seven, 'Cuddly' Dudley (Dudley Hessop), The King Brothers, Terry Dene, Lonnie Donegan, Alma Cogan, Don Lang, Shirley Bassey, Gerry Dorsey (later changed his name to Engelbert Humperdinck), Marion Ryan, Tony Sheridan.

Perry Mason (1957–66) BBC TV. This American legal drama series starred Raymond Burr as a fictional Los Angeles defence attorney, Perry Mason, who always won his cases. Perry would solve the cases with the help of his investigator, Paul Drake, played by William Hopper, and his confidential secretary, Della Street, played by Barbara Hale. They did it all by themselves, sometimes they even found the body! And of course the police and the district attorney always charged the wrong person with the crime. The drama would end with Perry Mason getting the real villain to break down in the courtroom's witness box and admit to having done it.

The Phil Silvers Show (1957–61) BBC TV. Phil Silvers played the fast-talking Sergeant Ernie Bilko in this American situation comedy in which Bilko and his subordinate team of soldiers undertake all sorts of get-rich-quick schemes behind the back of Colonel John T. Hall, played by Paul Ford, at the fictional Fort Baxter. Other cast members included Harvey Lembeck as Corporal Rocco Barbella, Allan Melvin as Corporal Steve Henshaw, Herbie

Faye as Private Sam Fender and Maurice Gosfield as the slovenly Private Duane Doberman.

Picture Book (1955–73) BBC TV. Part of the *Watch With Mother* series, created by Freda Lingstrom. Patricia Driscoll initially introduced *Picture Book*, but she left in 1957 to play the part of Maid Marian alongside Richard Green in the ITV series, *The Adventures of Robin Hood*. You will remember Patricia's soothing voice, and her catchphrase, 'Do you think you could do this? – I am sure you could if you tried'. Vera McKechnie replaced her and kept up the good work. Each Monday the picture book would be opened to reveal a drawing of a house, and the camera would take us through the window to set the scene for a story to be told.

The Pinky and Perky Show (1957) BBC TV. A pair of puppet pigs that wore different clothes but were indistinguishable on 1950s black and white televisions. Pinky and Perky spoke and sang in high-pitched squeaky voices, created from speeded-up recordings, and they performed comedy sketches. They became very popular in the 1960s.

Popeye! (The Sailor Man) (1958) ITV. The cartoon adventures of Popeye the sailor man, his girlfriend Olive Oyl and his love rival, the villainous brute Bluto. There was also the infant, Swee' Pea, who was found abandoned, and the hamburger-munching J. Wellington Wimpy. The adventures always involved a punch-up with Bluto, with Popeye eventually winning after gaining some extra muscular strength by swallowing a can of spinach. This show was a firm favourite with the kids.

Quatermass – The Quatermass Experiment (1953), *Quatermass II* (1955), and *Quatermass and the Pit* (1959) BBC TV. These science fiction dramas frightened the life out of everyone and sent kids to bed with nightmares. Aliens taking over the world, dramatised with eerie sound and visual effects. Very amateur by today's standards, but realistic enough for the 1950s.

Rag, Tag and Bobtail (1953–65) BBC TV. Part of the *Watch With Mother* series, produced by Freda Lingstrom using stories by Louise Cochrane, about the woodland adventures of a hedgehog, a mouse and a rabbit.

Robin Hood (The Adventures of Robin Hood) (1955–60) ITV. Weekly half-hour adventures of the legendary Robin Hood and his band of merry men who stole from the rich and gave to the poor in Sherwood Forest; starring Richard Green as Robin Hood, Alan Wheatley as The Sheriff of Nottingham, Archie Duncan as Little John, Bernadette O'Farrell and later Patricia Driscoll as Maid Marian, Alexander Gauge as Friar Tuck and Paul Eddington (later famous for his roles in *The Good Life*, *Yes Minister*, and *Yes Prime Minister*) as Will Scarlet. This was a hugely popular children's programme. The theme song was written by Carl Sigman and sung by Dick James – Robin Hood, Robin Hood, riding through the glen …

Sir Lancelot (1956–7) ITV. The adventures of Sir Lancelot du Lac, a knight of King Arthur's Round Table and Queen Guinevere's champion. In each of the thirty episodes we saw Sir Lancelot, played by William Russell, fight off the baddies and save his fellow knights from danger, and he was always there to rescue the queen or any princesses that might find themselves locked up in the tower.

Six-Five Special (1957–8) BBC TV. Britain's first rock and roll and jazz live music television programme, produced by Jack Good and presented by Pete Murray. It took its name from the time it was broadcast – five past six on Saturday evenings. Pete Murray, a hip thirty-two-year-old disc-jockey back then, littered his presentation with trendy 1950s words like square, cat, cool, gas, get with it and have a ball. The co-producer and narrator, Josephine Douglas, would translate Pete's trendy slang words for the benefit of any 1950s parents that might be watching the show. Regulars on the show included Kenny Baker and his Jazzmen, Michael Holliday, Bobbie and Rudy, and the King Brothers. Other guests included Petula Clarke, Jim Dale (went on to present the show), Terry Dene, Lonnie Donegan, Vince Eager, Johnny Dankworth, Russ Hamilton, Tubby Hayes, Cleo Lane, Don Lang, Freddie Mills, The Mudlarks, Joan Regan, Ronnie Scott and Marty Wilde. The show also included sport, news and comedy segments. Another essential watch for kids of all ages who wanted to see all the top artists of the day perform live.

The Sooty Show (1955–92) BBC TV. The yellow glove puppet bear with black nose and ears was devised by Harry Corbett in 1948 and first appeared on our screens in BBC TV's *Talent Night* in 1952. Sooty and Harry then became regulars on the BBC's children's show *Saturday Special* from 1952–5. In 1955 they were awarded their own show, *The Sooty Show*. In 1957, Harry introduced a friend for Sooty called Sweep, a dog with long ears and red nose (not that the colour mattered on black and white television). In 1967, *The Sooty Show* transferred from BBC to ITV, and Sooty with his magic wand continued to entertain kids with different presenters until 1992. 'Bye bye everyone! Bye bye!'

Sportsview (1954–68) BBC TV. This was the first television sports magazine programme, and Peter Dimmock

8.0 VAL PARNELL'S SUNDAY NIGHT AT THE LONDON PALLADIUM

One hour of entertainment from the world's most famous Variety Theatre

Starring

EARTHA KITT

with

FULL SUPPORTING STAR CAST

and

George Carden's London Palladium Girls The London Palladium Orchestra directed by Eric Rogers

This star-studded show is compered by

TOMMY TRINDER

who also introduces

BEAT THE CLOCK

America's most popular audience-participation show. Presented by arrangement with Goodson and Todman and C.B.S.

THE JACKPOT PRIZE

If not won January 20

WILL STAND AT £300

Produced by
VAL PARNELL
Directed for television by
STEPHEN WADE
An ATV Network Production

ITV's television line-up for Val Parnell's Sunday Night at the London Palladium on Sunday 27 January 1957.

presented it. Its most memorable sports coverage items included Roger Bannister's four-minute mile.

Sunday Night at the London Palladium (1955–67) ITV. British television variety show produced by Val Parnell. The regular 1950s hosts were Tommy Trinder (1955–8) and Bruce Forsyth (1958–60). There were also other hosts that stood in from time to time during this period, including Dickie Henderson, Alfred Marks, Bob Monkhouse and Robert Morley. Entertainment included the Tiller Girls, speciality acts, and guest artists like Gracie Fields, Bob Hope, Guy Mitchell and Johnny Ray. The middle of the show featured the popular game show *Beat the Clock*, in which members of the audience were invited to complete unusual tasks in a short period of time, measured by a large clock at the back of the stage. The show ended each week with all the guests assembled on a revolving stage.

Take Your Pick (1955–68) ITV. Quizmaster Michael Miles invited contestants to answer simple questions for 60 seconds without using the words Yes or No. Alec Dane stood next to him with a gong, ready to gong the contestant out if they said the forbidden words. If the contestant got through that round then they could select any key from one of thirteen boxes. Miles would offer them increasing amounts of money in exchange for the key. If the money didn't tempt the contestant then he or she went on to open their chosen box with the key. Three of the boxes would contain booby prizes and box 13 would contain a mystery prize. There was also a 'treasure chest of money' and a 'star prize', which was always a three-piece-suite ... ooooh!

This is Your Life (1955–64) BBC TV. Hosted by Eamonn Andrews with the 'red book', which each week was filled with a 'surprise' guest's life story. Andrews was himself the first unwitting victim of the show (he thought he was going to surprise Freddie Mills but the guest turned out to be Andrews himself). There were just a few that rejected the surprise, most notably footballer Danny Blanchflower in 1961, who didn't take kindly to the invasion of his privacy and just walked off.

Torchy, the Battery Boy (1958–9) ITV. The adventures of Torchy, the puppet boy who is powered by battery, and his friends in Topsy-Turvy Land. The series was produced by AP Films and Gerry Anderson (he of later *Thunderbirds* fame) at a time when you could still see the puppet's strings.

Tugboat Annie (*The Adventures of Tugboat Annie*) (1957–61) ITV. 'Tugboat' Annie was the widowed captain of the tugboat *Narcissus*. The stories revolved around the rivalry between 'Tugboat' Annie Brennan, played by Minerva Urecal, and her long time rival, Captain Horatio Bullwinkle, played by Walter Sande, captain of the *Salamander*. They each did all they could to hinder the other's activities, trading insults all the way.

Twizzle (*The Adventures of Twizzle*) (1957–8) ITV Associated Rediffusion. Twizzle was a boy doll that could extend its arms and legs to be 'as tall as a lamppost' by twizzling them. The series started with Twizzle running away from a toy shop to avoid being bought for two shillings by a horrid little girl. Twizzle met lots of new friends and had a series of fun adventures. His first new friend was Footso the black cat who helped him build Stray Town where stray toys could live safely, away from owners that mistreated them. Other friends included Jiffy the Broomstick Man, Chawky the white-faced Golliwog, Polly

Moppet, Candy Floss, and Bouncy the ball that had lost its bounce. The series was made by AP Films, Arthur Provis and Gerry Anderson's newly formed independent production company. They had a long way to go in television puppetry, what with all those jerky movements and thick strings that were as visible as the puppets themselves.

Wagon Train (1958–65) ITV. Very popular hour-long western series, starring Ward Bond as wagon master Major Seth Adams, and Robert Horton as Flint McCullough. You will probably also remember old Charlie Wooster, the comical cook, played by Frank McGrath. Each week, the wagon train team managed to save some pioneering settlers from the Indians as they made their way through the endless deserts and rocky mountain passes in covered wagons. Lots of exciting horseback chases, with loads of guest stars.

Watch With Mother (1952–73) BBC TV. Created by Freda Lingstrom as television's answer to radio's *Listen With Mother*. Originally known as *For The Children*, which had been on television since before the war and first introduced us to *Muffin The Mule* in 1946, *Watch With Mother* brought together a daily sequence of programmes aimed at preschool children, including *Picture Book* (on Mondays from 1955), *Andy Pandy* (on Tuesdays from 1950), *Flowerpot Men* (on Wednesdays from 1952), *Rag, Tag and Bobtail* (on Thursdays from 1953), and *The Woodentops* (on Fridays from 1955). *See separate programme headings for more details about these shows.*

Whack-O! (1956–60) BBC TV. British comedy sitcom series, written by Frank Muir and Denis Norden, and starring Jimmy Edwards as Professor James Edwards MA,

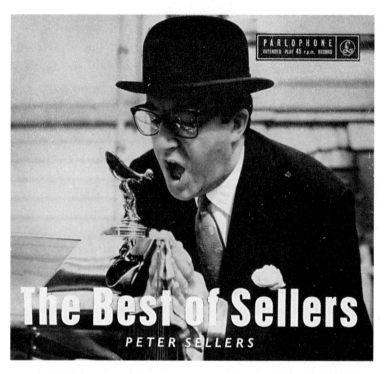

Peter Sellers kept us all laughing throughout the '50s as one of the Goons on BBC Radio's *Goon Show*, and with his comedy appearances on other radio shows like *Ray's a Laugh* and *Workers Playtime*.

a scheming, gambling, drunken, cane-wielding headmaster of fictional Chiselbury public school. The show also starred Arthur Howard, who played Professor Edwards' long-suffering assistant, Mr Oliver Pettigrew. You may remember Professor Edwards' favourite saying, 'Bend over, Wendover!'

The Woodentops (1955–7) BBC TV. Part of the *Watch With Mother* series, written by Maria Bird. It was about a family of wooden dolls who lived on a farm. The main characters were Mummy Woodentop, Daddy Woodentop, Jenny, Willy and Baby Woodentop. The series was devised to introduce children to the ways of the country.

Zoo Time (1956–68) ITV. Featured Desmond Morris, with the help of various animal experts and zoo staff from Regents Park Zoo in London. It offered lots of information about animals, using pictures taken from around the zoo. The early shows always featured Congo the chimpanzee.

Seven

SCHOOL LIFE

Your first day at school; it was the loneliest day of your young life. You were just four years old when your mum took you into the school, kissed you on the cheek, then turned and walked away, leaving you alone and abandoned. There were no working-class nursery schools, kindergartens or playschools to prepare you for the distress you felt that day. Up until that moment, you had always followed in your mum's shadow. You had never before been left alone with strangers and you are suddenly forced to realise that your mum had always done everything for you. For the first time in your life, adults that you don't even know are asking you questions and telling you to do things, and your mum isn't there to deal with it for you. You are in strange surroundings that are filled with odd smells, and there are unfamiliar things all around you, with lots of kids that you have never seen before. Your mum had taught you to be well-behaved but you weren't prepared for the discipline of school life. The teacher shows you to your seat and tells you to sit still and be quiet. This is not going to be any fun at all – and where are all the toys?

Many schools had a school uniform policy, which was designed to be affordable and could also be worn outside school. Girls' uniforms were often just a white blouse, grey gymslip or pinafore dress, white socks and navy blue knickers – girls never wore trousers to school. Boys would wear a white or grey shirt and short grey flannel trousers with itchy long grey ribbed woollen socks – with at least one uncomfortable darned toe. There was frequently a school tie and some schools also had very tasteful headgear as part of the uniform. Both boys and girls would wear a blazer that often doubled as a best jacket for the boys to wear on Sundays. School shoes were generally heavy black round-toed monstrosities that were nicknamed 'fish-boxes', and there were black plimsolls for games and PE (physical education). As a rule, it was a bit uncool for boys to wear raincoats or overcoats, but girls regularly wore them. These coats were always bought two sizes too big to allow for growth and to give at least a couple of years' wear; and because they were indistinguishable they all had the owner's name neatly sewn into the collar.

If you lived in a rural area, you may have travelled by school bus or train, but most 1950s kids walked to school and some lucky ones cycled, sometimes quite long distances. Very young children were escorted to school by one of their parents, but once they knew how to get there then most children made their own way to school, particularly if they had older siblings or friends to accompany them. The streets were safer then, and you never heard of children being abducted. Walking to and from school could in itself be an adventure; running alongside cars and trying to keep up with them, hopping from flagstone to flagstone while avoiding every crack, running along the tops of walls, climbing trees, and the annual ritual of collecting conkers that fell from the horse-chestnut trees every autumn.

You had to pay to go by bus unless you lived a qualifying distance from the school, whereby you got a bus pass. In the towns and cities, with car ownership still relatively low, trolleybuses were the main means of transport to school for children that lived too far away to walk. Travelling by bus was quite different then; everyone queued in an orderly line at the bus stop and there was no pushing or shoving to get to the front. If there was a bend in the road, or a hill that was obscuring your view of oncoming traffic, then you could tell when a trolleybus was approaching by looking at the movement of the overhead wires, to which the spring-loaded trolley-poles on top of the buses were connected. Or, you could put your ear against the post at the bus stop and listen to the increasing vibrations. Experience taught you just how far away the bus was depending upon how much the wires were moving. You would always go upstairs on the bus for a better view, and it was even better if you could get a seat at the front, but it was always very smoky because people were only allowed to smoke upstairs on the buses.

'Hold very tight please', ding-ding. There was a uni-formed conductor on every bus whose job it was to collect fares and to make sure everyone got on and off the bus safely. There was no passenger door on buses, just an opening at the back with an upright centre pole for you to cling to as you got on and off. The conductor carried a long narrow wad of different-priced tickets, from which he or she would pull a ticket and clip it before handing it to you. They would always take your money, count it and then put it in their leather moneybag before handing you the ticket. Sometimes the conductor would take your money just as the bus was arriving at a bus stop, which meant that they had to go to the back of the bus to supervise passengers getting on and off the bus – it seemed they would always forget to come back with your ticket!

In the 1950s, even the infant school had strict discipline. The classroom was geared to learning, not playing. There was no sign of a cuddly toy or hint of an afternoon nap. The teachers did adopt a more gentle touch for the infants, but talking in class, fidgeting or not paying attention would lead to a slap across the legs and being made to stand in the corner of the classroom facing the wall. Punishment would undoubtedly upset you, but there was also a new feeling that you had never felt before – you had been shown up in front of the other kids. That 'new feeling' was humiliation. Once you got used to the discipline of being at infant school, you found that there were lots of fun things to do, and the teachers actually made learning enjoyable!

The school day was normally seven hours long, including lunch and break times. The starting and finishing times varied from school to school, with starting times from 8.40–9.10 am and finishing times from 3.40–4.10 pm. Most schools had morning assembly, which more often than not included prayers, and then you went off to your classroom for the register to be checked.

You usually transferred into the junior or primary school proper between the ages of five and six, by which time you

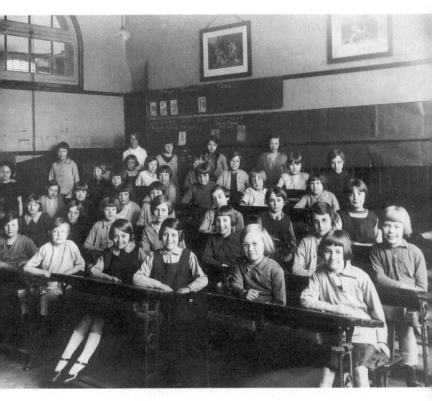

A classroom full of young schoolgirls sitting at typical 1950s metal-framed desks with sloped desktops that are fitted with inkwells.

knew your alphabet and could do basic arithmetic with the aid of an abacus. You gradually progressed from writing with chalk on a small blackboard to using pencils, and when you had mastered the use of a pencil you were taught to write with pen and ink. This involved using a crude wooden stick with a metal nib fixed to one end, which you dipped into an inkwell at the top of your desk to load the nib with enough ink to write a couple of words at a time.

It was really messy! There would be ink everywhere, with splodges all over the pages in your exercise book and on your hands. Loading just the right amount of ink onto the nib was the key, and it helped if you had an undamaged nib to start with.

Class sizes varied considerably depending on where you lived. People often had large families and in the built-up areas it was quite normal to have more than forty children to a class. Sometimes a classroom could not accommodate enough desks, which meant that some had to share. If seated at the back of a large class, a quiet or shy child with poor eyesight or hearing could go unnoticed by the teacher and struggle to keep up with lessons – sometimes harshly branded as being lazy! Teachers back then probably weren't trained to identify such problems, and some were less than sympathetic with children that didn't conform to what was seen as the norm, as with their criticism of left-handed kids who were often encouraged or even forced to write with their right hand, sometimes earning a slap on the back of the hand if they were seen writing left-handed.

Some schools had a daily ritual of dishing out cod liver oil to all youngsters, but in other schools cod liver oil was only given to certain unlucky individuals; this was never really explained but it did seem to be linked to sickly looking kids and those on free school meals. Similarly, some kids had their hair more regularly checked for nits than others. Yes, alas, we all had regular inspections by the 'nit nurse'! There were also regular school medical inspections, when a doctor would visit the school and you would all line up to be examined. It was usually a male doctor and he would pull you about, checking you all over, then weigh you, measure your height, and make you do things like pick up a pencil using your toes. Everyone hated the 'nit nurse' and doctor inspections.

Apart from having fun, your main ambition at primary school was to be made a 'monitor'. Any kind of monitor would do. You will remember everyone putting their hands up in class to volunteer when there were pencils or paintbrushes to be given out, and the collective call of 'Me Miss! – Me Miss!' As well as giving out the pencils, the pencil monitor got to use the huge pencil sharpener that was mounted on the edge of teacher's desk at the front of the class – how exciting! It was recognition of your trustworthiness and you felt quite important to be given the responsibility of teacher's little helper. Milk monitor was a rotten job; you didn't put your hand up twice to be the milk monitor. Remember those small bottles (one-third of a pint) of free school milk you had each morning throughout your school life? Nice and refreshing in summer, but very cold in winter. The milk monitor had to handle all those freezing cold milk bottles and the metal crates they came in. The job of class monitor was best suited to girls because it involved having to 'tell' on your classmates if they misbehaved when teacher was out of the classroom. Not that girls were better at telling tales, it's just that boys didn't usually last long in the job; they would at best be ostracised by their mates in the playground if they got someone in trouble with the teacher.

There were lots of fun things to do in class, like drawing, painting, and making things with plasticine and other materials. Everything you did would be given a mark out of ten, and little stick-on coloured, silver and gold stars would be awarded for good work. You were also taught the basics in science and nature, but the majority of class time was spent on learning 'the three Rs', a long-established phrase that was used to describe the basic skills of reading, writing and arithmetic. You were never in any doubt that school was a place for learning.

There were very few male primary school teachers around at the time. The teachers were mainly women and most appeared to be very old, but then again, to a child anyone over the age of twenty-one looked old, and I suppose they did in the 1950s. On the other hand, every primary school did seem to have just one nice-looking young schoolteacher that everyone wanted to have as their class teacher. Children would describe their teacher as nice, horrible, or all right, without realising the true value of that teacher, good or bad, until later in their young lives. As in every generation, the 1950s primary school teachers had varying levels of knowledge and teaching skills. Some were lazy and boring, limiting themselves to teaching the basic three Rs, whereas others were true vocational teachers that involved themselves in every aspect of teaching; attending after-school courses to learn additional things like drama, painting, handicrafts and music. If you were lucky enough to have had one of those enterprising primary school teachers then you will appreciate the contribution that he or she made to your development. They made schoolwork enjoyable for their pupils and provided a complete mix of education. It was usually the same resourceful teachers that took you for swimming lessons at the local baths, arranged needlework and dance classes for the girls, and taught the boys how to play football and cricket properly. He or she would have been there when you were given your first tambourine or triangle to hit as part of the enthusiastic but shambolic school orchestra; and who was it that taught you how to breathe when you practised for the school choir's Christmas carol concert? On cold winter days, your teacher sat at the front of the class and bewitched you with readings from children's fictional story books, or fascinated you with tales of British history; the ancient Egyptian mummies, The Battle of Hastings in 1066, King John and The Magna Carta of 1215. It made you feel warm inside, and even though playtime was fast approaching you didn't want the story to end.

Your teacher taught you how to mould plasticine and cover the moulding with papier mâché, made from torn-up bits of old newspaper stuck together in layers using wet paste. You learnt a variety of crafts from painting pictures and murals to making collages, and talented teachers even taught things like basket weaving. In summer, your teacher would have been there on the school sports day to help prepare you for the sack race, the egg and spoon and wheelbarrow races; and in winter, he or she would have been there to encourage you on those awful muddy cross-country runs.

Why was it that you were always dragged out on the coldest and wettest winter day to do a cross-country run? And it always seemed to be cold and wet on the days you went to the swimming baths, with everyone shivering away in those poolside changing huts – or cupboards more like!

It was your class teacher that decorated the classroom with Christmas decorations and organised your school Christmas party where you were taught how to play party games like pass the parcel, musical chairs and blind man's buff. The teacher would bring records in from home to play during the party. Christmas songs like The Beverley Sisters' *Little Drummer Boy* and Harry Belafonte's *Mary's Boy Child*, as well as some pop songs like Cliff Richard's *Living Doll* and Tommy Steele's *Singing the Blues*.

From playing with small beanbags in the school hall to your first game of rounders in the playground, and even dressing up for a part in the Christmas nativity play, your primary school teacher showed you how to do it all … and still managed to teach you 'the three Rs'!

In the 1950s, the cost of school dinners was subsidised by the government. The contribution made by parents had gradually increased during the previous decade so that by 1957 parents were paying a shilling a day for each of their children's school dinners. Your class teacher would collect the week's 'five-bob' school dinner money when calling the register on a Monday morning. It always delayed the start of lessons by several minutes because little Johnny couldn't find all his money, and little Mary had forgotten hers completely – no wait! She's found it, safely wrapped in a handkerchief and tucked up inside the leg of her navy blue knickers. Then the teacher had to deal with those children from families on very low incomes that qualified for free school dinners. Even through the eyes of a child, it was uncomfortable to see individual classmates singled out as being poor – every Monday morning!

Some kids just couldn't stomach the thought of eating school dinners and so they would keep their school dinner money to spend on other things and pretend to the teacher that they were going home for lunch. After all, no child can surely forget the horrible smell of boiled vegetables that engulfed the school buildings around lunchtime, or the taste of whatever was in that meat pie you had to eat, and the semolina pudding for afters – yuck!

Playground Games and Mischief

There was always a lot of fun and tomfoolery going on in primary school playgrounds. In the morning before school started, and at break times, they were a hive of activity, with girls and boys competing for space to play all sorts of ball and chase games. Boys would mark out the best stretch of fence as a goal for their football game, while girls would bagsy any piece of high wall to play two-balls against. In summer, cricket and rounders would join the array of ball games being played and there would be balls flying everywhere, with many hitting innocent young bystanders. In autumn, although ball games remained popular, conkers was the dominant game, with small conker tournaments taking place all over the playground. The game required intense concentration and was only interrupted by the occasional wipe of a dripping nose with a coat sleeve. There was a lot of cruel teasing between kids in the playground. Anything that made you different would be targeted for name-calling during squabbles. It could be the colour of your hair or the braces on your teeth; nothing was safe in the war of words - four-eyes, ginger, lanky, fatso, snotty, anything that could be used to caricature a temporary rival. And that's what they often were, very short-lived enemies who would be playing happily with you five minutes later.

The school caretaker would often bring quarrels to a halt as he made his way across the playground with a bucket of sand, which he was forever carting around the school to cover a freshly deposited heap of vomit in one of the school corridors.

Generally, you weren't allowed to go out to the lavatory during class time, and since there was never any toilet paper in the lavatories you quickly learned to hold onto anything other than pee until you got home in the evening. By the time breaktime arrived, bladders were full and there was always a queue for the loo. Unless you were in a newly built school, all the lavatories were situated in the playground. They had no roofs, and sit-downs had no locks on the doors, if any doors at all – alfresco, you might say! It was because of those bulging bladders that young boys quickly discovered the 'boys only' school lavatory game of 'highest up the wall'!

Skipping ropes were always in use somewhere in the playground, with groups of girls chanting rhymes with key words and phrases that prompted the skipper to do certain skipping tricks. The girls loved those rhymes. Rope skipping, French (elastics) skipping and ball juggling games were all done to rhymes. Young girls would often be seen forming circles to play rhyming games and sometimes they would just stand around singing.

Ring a-ring o'roses,
A pocketful of posies.
A-tishoo! A-tishoo!
We all fall down.

London Bridge is falling down,
Falling down, falling down.
London Bridge is falling down,
My fair lady.

Baa, baa, black sheep, have you any wool?
Yes sir, yes sir, three bags full,
One for the master, one for the dame,
And one for the little boy who lives down the lane.

Christmas is coming, the geese are getting fat
Please put a penny in the old man's hat;
If you haven't got a penny, a ha'penny will do,
If you haven't got a ha'penny then God bless you!

Cry Baby Bunting
Daddy's gone a-hunting,
Gone to fetch a rabbit skin
To wrap the Baby Bunting in
Cry Baby Bunting.

The tuck shop came back into full use after sweet rationing ended on Wednesday 4 February 1953. All sorts of penny chews and tiny packets of sweets went back on sale at school tuck shops throughout the country. It was the first time in their young lives that schoolchildren had known the delight of a fully stocked tuck shop; after all, sweets had been subject to rationing since 1942. The tuck shop was open during mid-morning break, but money was still scarce and many schoolchildren could only stand and admire the delights on offer. Those that did have some coppers jangling in their pockets usually went for their favourite loose sweets that were sold in ones and twos, and cost very little. Aniseed balls and malted milk tablets were very popular because they had strong flavours and you could suck them for ages. The malted milk tablets were like the Horlicks tablets that were sold in chemist shops at ninepence for a small tin.

Eleven-Plus Exam

Everything you learned at primary school was in preparation for the eleven-plus exams, which you took soon after your eleventh birthday. You were used to being given a set of sums to calculate, or a composition to write for English, but you had never before experienced an examination. Your parents and teachers drummed the importance of the exam into you, and everyone got very nervous about it. The eleven-plus examination was used to determine which type of school you were most suited to go to later that year when you finished at primary school. The idea was that different skills required different schooling and the exam was intended to determine whether you were best suited to a grammar school, a secondary modern school, or a technical school. This was a life-changing event for which you had sole responsibility, and sadly, the result could only go one of two ways – 'pass' and you were an academic success and going on to grammar school, or failure, which meant you were going to a secondary modern school with the prospects of leaving school at fifteen with little or no qualifications unless you went on to college. Many kids had no real understanding of what the differences were between grammar and secondary modern schools. They just wanted to go to the nearest school because they didn't fancy the thought of travelling, or to the same school as their elder sibling, and many were happy just as long as they went to the same school as their classmates.

On the morning of the exam, there was a real air of importance and secrecy that you had never known before. You did the exams with all your classmates under teacher supervision in your own classroom. You were told not to talk to anyone, pass messages, or look around at all until after the examination was over. The examination question papers were placed upside down on your desk in front of you, and at the appointed hour, when the papers had all been distributed, you were told to turn the papers over and begin.

The exam was in three parts, arithmetic and problem solving, general English (including comprehension and an essay), and general knowledge. Try these two c. 1950s eleven-plus-exam questions:

Q1. A motorist leaves home at 10.15am and drives at 32 miles per hour. He stops for lunch from noon to 1.45pm and then continues his journey at 30 miles per hour. How many miles has he travelled by 5pm?

Q2. Simplify the fractions ⅘ - ⁷⁄₁₀

Remember this was for eleven-year-olds; there were no calculators and you had to show all your workings-out on the paper, including crossings-out, and children were mainly taught to use fractions rather than decimals when doing calculations.

A1. 153½
A2. ⅒

The method of revealing eleven-plus exam results left a lot to be desired. Many schools just read them out after morning assembly, creating an atmosphere of great tension and distress among the children. It was a moment of great joy to the few lucky ones that passed, but it left some of those who failed absolutely distraught, particularly as it was sometimes left for them to tell their parents the news. The saddest thing of all was seeing some of the cleverest kids in the class fail. It can only be down to nerves that they failed, but it was heartbreaking for them to learn that the results of one morning's tests had been used to judge whether or not they were academically qualified for grammar school. Once the emotions of the results day had calmed down, there was then the overwhelming realisation that friends were going to be split up and sent to different schools. Some that lived a distance apart might never see each other again. However, passing the eleven-plus did not in itself guarantee entry to a grammar school.

Secondary Schools

All grammar schools and some secondary modern schools required applicants to attend selection interviews from which the school would pick the best of the bunch. Parents would be required to select and list three schools in the order of their preference, and that list would come into play if you were turned down by your first choice school. It was rumoured that schools didn't look too kindly upon applicants who had listed their school as being third choice. The school interview was the second-biggest life-changing occurrence in your young life over which you had influence. It would determine whether or not you were to go to your school of choice.

Whatever school you ended up in, you then had to come to terms with being one of the new kids – what a turn of events! After all, you had come from the comfortable and familiar surroundings of your primary school, which, after some seven years, had earned you position and respect as one of the 'top dogs' in the playground, and now you had been instantly relegated to being among the smallest, weakest and dumbest in this new and unfamiliar playground. The whole ethos was different. You were now surrounded by huge spotty youths with attitude, whose main occupation during break times was to stand around in groups talking, and some might even use you as sport for bullying. To protect yourself, you soon learnt that there was safety in numbers. Some of those gravel-voiced teenagers towering over you were like fully grown adults, with chin stubble and everything – and they were just the girls!

Within days of joining your new school you began to feel much older, and with the task of survival high on your agenda, the childish games of old were soon erased from your mind. You had to contend with 'sums' becoming mathematics, the learning of foreign languages, world history and geography, boys doing woodwork, domestic science for girls, but then there was the exciting possibility of learning how to make stink bombs in the chemistry laboratory. Many had to deal with the disappointment of being placed in a single-sex school, and if you went to a grammar school then there was the additional burden of having to learn confusing subjects like economics and Latin. And then there was the homework! You were set loads of homework to do, which was a complete shock to the system; it took up most of the evening and completely changed your way of life, particularly grammar school homework, which covered several more academic subjects. The old routine of school, tea, play, relax, and then to bed, quickly turned into a new routine of school, tea, homework and bed. And on top of that, some had to fit an hour's school detention and visits to the library into their evening's schedule as well! Yes, part of your schoolwork and homework required that you make regular visits to the local library to look up information in reference books. This was a time when the word 'computer' wasn't yet used in everyday language, and even commercial computers, which were the size of a room, were rare. The hand-held pocket calculator hadn't yet been invented, and all mathematical calculations were done using pen and paper with just the aid of your brain. From a very young age you were taught your times tables (multiplication tables), and were constantly tested on your ability to recite them and answer on-the-spot questions put to you. Maths teachers would randomly point at individuals around the class and fire questions at them – Nine eights? Twelve sevens? Eleven fours?

At school, you did loads of physical education and sport, with hard-working PE sessions two or three days a week, and typically there would be a weekly games afternoon for competitive sports like football, rugby, cricket, rounders, tennis, hockey, netball, and not forgetting athletics. There was also extra training after school, and school league competitions were held on Saturdays. Just to be sure that you used up every spare ounce of energy, some schools even taught and competed in additional sports like boxing, judo and weightlifting.

Everything was so different at secondary school; what with your new friends and a much heavier workload, you just didn't have time to look back at your primary school days. You were gradually leaving your childhood behind and moving ever closer to becoming a moody teenager.

Corporal Punishment

Corporal or physical punishment, the act of inflicting pain by means of beating or caning, was legal and widely practised in Britain's schools during the 1950s. At the time, the psychological effects of physical punishment on children was not considered as adding to the punishment, but anyone who experienced corporal punishment in school will know that the suffering was not limited to the pain felt at the moment of impact. You would often know in advance that you were to be caned, and this would cause a build-up of mental anguish that would today be regarded as cruel. Being punished in front of the class or school would be humiliating and add significantly to your mental suffering. Then there was the after effect, with the extra stress of hiding it from your parents – the unwritten law of the playground was 'not to tell tales out of school'; and of course you didn't want them to find out anyway or you might get another wallop for having misbehaved at school in the first place. The actual pain of the cane or tawse could last for several hours, with welts and bruises remaining evident for days.

In primary schools, physical punishment was mostly limited to a slap using the palm of the hand across the back of your legs, arms, or hands, and sometimes the back of the head. A wooden ruler was also used to administer a rap across the knuckles, hands, or back of the legs. The cane, slipper, or tawse (in Scotland) was usually reserved for older primary school boys. There was no negotiation or appeals; if in doubt give the child a clout!

Corporal punishment was much more prevalent in secondary schools, but again, predominantly for boys, although you did hear stories of girls being slapped with a slipper or caned. Boys' schools sometimes had designated 'punishment rooms', with specially appointed 'punishment teachers' to do the wicked deed. There is no doubt that the use of corporal punishment in schools was practised with great enthusiasm by some cruel and cowardly teachers who took pleasure in beating even the frailest of young boys. Although schools were supposed to keep records of any corporal punishment they dished out, in what were called 'punishment books', the rule was not adhered to and punishment would often be meted out on the spur of the moment, and sometimes at random with the teacher not even knowing who was being beaten, or losing count of the number of strokes being landed on the target. Clouts across the back of the head for not paying attention were commonplace, and there was an unending supply of chalk, blackboard dusters and other missiles thrown across the classroom as instant recognition of someone's misbehaviour.

All forms of discipline were seen as a natural part of the education process, and physical punishment was even considered to be 'character building'!

Eight

SCHOOL HOLIDAYS

Every day off school was greatly valued, as it seemed that you spent an awful lot of your time there. Apart from the traditional six weeks summer holiday, other school breaks were short and scarce. There were no special days off, as with the 'occasional days', 'teacher training days', and 'non-pupil days' of today. Half-term breaks were often limited to two days, with Easter and Christmas extended to one full week, and that included the official public holidays. If you went sick during term time then you might get a visit from the school board man to check up on you (most people didn't have telephones back then). Truancy was frowned upon and strictly dealt with – there were what was called 'school board men' that would lurk around neighbourhoods to catch kids bunking off school. If you were caught then you would be dragged back to school for punishment, and your parents would get a visit and a lecture from the school board man, threatening all sorts of things, including the possibility of you being sent to borstal if you were caught again. There were different expressions used to describe skipping-off school depending on what part of the country you lived in. These included 'hopping the wag', 'wagging it', 'playing the wag' and 'skiving off'. Of course, it was only the very bad kids that did it!

Most working adults only got two weeks paid holiday a year, with part-timers and piece-workers getting no holiday pay at all. They often had to take their holiday at a time determined by their employer, such as during factory closedown periods. This was usually in the main summer months, and so families that could afford it would try to get away for a few days during the school summer break. It was only the well-off that went away on holidays at other times of the year.

Seaside Holidays

Cheap European package holidays and affordable long haul flights to exotic places didn't exist in the '50s, and the thought of spending a fortnight's holiday on a sun-soaked Greek island was way beyond your wildest dreams. Here in Britain, the 'Hi-di-Hi!' style holiday camps at popular seaside resorts were all heaving with fun-loving, knobbly knee contestants, and game-playing holidaymakers. All the caravan sites, seaside chalets and beach huts were also full to the brim, as were the traditional seaside boarding houses. Not everyone could afford to go away on holiday. It was in the days before credit cards arrived in Britain, so people had to have the cash available to pay for a holiday, otherwise they just couldn't go. Many working-class families strived to

A group of children wearing sagging, wet bathing suits play in the shallow water on a Fife beach in 1951.

save enough money to have a modest seaside holiday, and to get some healthy sea air into their kids' lungs. If you were lucky enough to go on holiday, then it was likely to consist of a week at one of the popular seaside towns around the country, with sticks of rock, 'naughty' postcards, donkey rides, and 'kiss me quick' hats.

In 1950, buses and bicycles were the most popular modes of transport. At the time, there were just under 2 million cars registered in Britain, with only 14 per cent of households owning a car (by 1998, it was 70 per cent). In summer, many families did load their luggage into the boot of a classic motor car of the day, like the Ford Prefect 100E Deluxe or the Austin A35 Saloon, but most families headed off to the nearest railway station to catch a train that took them right to the doorstep of their holiday destination. It was in the days before the Beeching 'Axe' Report (1963), which accelerated the mass closure of railway branch lines all across the country, at a time when you could still access small holiday resorts by train. The train journey created an atmosphere of excitement, as you trundled past the advertising hoardings and the grimy soot-stained walls that encased the railway station, out through the built-up areas and into the beautiful countryside. The panoramic view from the train revealed a countryside scene that was so different, and really eye-catching. You were mesmerised by the ever-changing landscape combined with the rhythmic motion of the train. You passed through all sorts of tiny village railway stations, deep into unfamiliar rural areas, way beyond the safety of your home turf. As captivated as you were by the moving scenery, you eventually got fed up fiddling with the adjustable leather window strap and began to ask the inevitable question – 'When will we be there?'

The beach huts, boarding houses and caravan sites were boring places for children, but kids of the '50s were used to finding things to occupy their time, and would do what they did at home – make up games, but on the beach rather than in the streets. Parents weren't into finding things to entertain the kids. After all, they had gone away for a rest as well, and there were no deep pockets full of cash with which to wander endlessly around amusement arcades, feeding the slot machines.

Casual wear was not something that grown-ups did very well in the 1950s. Men wore their everyday jacket and trousers to the beach, complete with shirt, tie, socks and shoes. They might stretch to a pair of brown sandals, but they would always be worn with socks! Your dad was really 'cool' if he wore a cotton t-shirt, or a patterned short-sleeve shirt. Once on the beach, he would take off his jacket and roll up his shirtsleeves, just to give the appearance of being laid-back. After fighting for several minutes to get the folding deckchair to open, he would settle down into it and don his knotted white hankie to protect his head from the sun. Some time later, he might take off his shoes and socks, roll up his trousers, and venture down the beach to dip a toe into the cold seawater that was lapping the shoreline. Brave dads even changed into swimming trunks and shivered their way down into the sea for a swim. Women commonly wore their best flowery summer dress to the beach, and maybe some white sandals for comfort, but it was not unusual to see women stumbling across the beach in three-inch high-heel shoes. There were a wide variety of swimsuit colours and styles for women, but although the daring two-piece bikini had been around for some time, there wasn't much evidence of it on Britain's beaches. Bikinis were mostly worn by beautiful Hollywood stars and jet-setters on beaches in the South of France. In Britain, we were a bit slow on the uptake. Perhaps it was our weather that made the ladies favour a one-piece, zip-up, corset-style swimsuit, with the essential modesty apron across the top of the legs to hide the swimsuit's crotch area. They were made in various fabrics and looked great until they got wet, retaining the

A group of children enjoy a donkey ride on the beach at Weston-super-Mare in the summer of 1955.

water and forming into a much less attractive shape. With all their fashionably permed hair and bouffants, women liked to protect their hair from getting wet in the water, and so they donned colourful rubber bathing caps that were lavishly decorated with designs of flowers, petals and shell-like shapes. Young girls commonly wore seersucker swimsuits, and even woollen knitted swimsuits that sagged down to the knees when they got wet.

A few days later, with all of the penny arcades, Punch and Judy shows, paddling pools and funfair rides done; and stuffed full of candy floss, whelks, fish and chips, and jellied eels, it's time to pack up and head for home to see your friends and enjoy the rest of the school holidays. One last peek at the saucy picture postcards outside the shops along the seafront, and you're off.

Holiday Time at Home

The summer holidays were so much more enjoyable than short half-term breaks. You had much more time for playing outside, getting up to mischief and making new friends. You had the good weather and light evenings, which meant more time for street games, and you were able to take whole days out to do things that you usually couldn't do, like go fishing, go to a roller-skating or ice-skating rink, or swimming at the nearest lido. If you had enough money, you might even go to a fairground or some other summer event, like a county cricket match. There were loads of things to do, and if you were broke you could still go to the park with your mates to kick a ball around, climb trees, or sail your homemade toy wooden boat on the lake. When you tired of playing, you could lie down in the fields to soak up the sun and make daisy chains.

Holiday or not, there was no rest for the wicked – your mum still got you out of bed at the crack of dawn, which meant you had long days to fill. There was a lot of unsupervised playtime during the holidays because dads were out at work all day, and a lot of mums also went out to work, either full- or part-time. Even mums that didn't go out to work seemed always to be busy indoors, with endless washing, ironing, cooking and cleaning. There were very few labour-saving devices in the average home, and most of these household jobs were done manually, which was really hard work.

It was a safer and more trusting time, when children were allowed to play out in the streets and around the neighbourhood without parents getting unduly worried. As long as you were out in a group, then you did things together and looked after each other.

Some of your most memorable summer days were spent out in the open, playing doorstep games in the sunshine. Games like Monopoly went on for hours and gave you a lot of enjoyment; it was educational in many ways, not least because it taught you how to add up. Card games were regularly played outside, on someone's doorstep or on a patch of grass, sometimes just for fun but often for a stake – rarely money, more often for matchsticks or something that was tradeable, like cigarette cards or marbles. Most kids knew how to play lots of card games, usually having learnt them from friends and relatives on dark winter evenings around the dining table, before television became the main form of entertainment in the home.

There weren't many cars or other motor vehicles around in the '50s, and a lot of back-streets were completely free of them, making them ideal playgrounds. A few lucky kids had bicycles, and long streets and alleyways were perfect for bicycle races, where boys and girls would take turns in racing the bikes against each other. Sometimes the races got dangerous, like when you competed to see how many you could fit on a bike at one time, and still ride it. Five was about the limit – saddle, crossbar, handlebar, and front and back mudguards. These antics often resulted in some bumps and scrapes, and the kids sometimes got hurt as well!

During the holidays you took each day as it came, knowing that tomorrow was another holiday, and the day after was another, and so on. Very little was planned in advance. You didn't listen to, or worry about the weather forecast. If it rained, then you tried to play somewhere under cover. Boys might retreat to a mate's house to construct some Meccano, or play Subbuteo, while girls were content to play dress-up with their mum's clothes and make-up, indoors. If you were stuck for something to do, then you went up to the high street to check out what was new in Woolworths. They always had something that you hadn't seen before, like the latest in wind-up toy cars. The girls spent ages looking through the range of cheap costume jewellery – a beaded necklace was only 1s 3d (one shilling and threepence). Woolworths had things that you didn't see anywhere else. At the time, it was the only place where you could buy Rupert the Bear Annuals. The pick 'n' mix counter was one of the biggest temptations, and best avoided. If you were spotted hanging around the sweet counter, you got chucked out. They knew you were just sheltering from the rain and weren't in there to buy anything.

Some unfortunate kids had school dinners arranged for them during the holidays, which meant that whatever they were doing, they had to stop at lunchtime and go off to the school for an hour. You always felt sorry for them, because although they were on holiday, they were unable to completely forget about school, having to go in through the school gates every day and see the same old school dinner ladies. Yes, it was very sad – everyone else could put school out of their heads for six whole weeks – that is, unless you were old enough to be at grammar school, because grammar school kids were given loads of homework to do during the school holidays. Most of them saved it all up to do near the end of the holidays, which meant that you didn't see much of them during the final week before the schools went back.

Sometimes, one or two of the mums would round up the neighbouring kids and take them off to the country or seaside for a day trip. It wasn't a task to be repeated more than once in any one summer holiday period; those mums needed the patience of a saint, as well as a firm hand – and a well-earned lie down when they got home. Perhaps these familiar words still echo in your ears: 'Never again!'

Much time during the school holidays was well spent and industrious; it wasn't all playtime. You spent a lot of time making things, mainly out of old bits of wood, like go-karts made out of old crates and prams, and sledges with removable ball-bearing wheels, which allowed them to be used in the concrete streets of summer, and on the snowy hills come wintertime. Then there was pocket money to be made out of collecting old newspapers, bottles and metals, and taking them down to the scrapyard for recycling. Towards the end of the summer holidays, thoughts would include plans for the next big event of the year, Bonfire Night. Gathering wood, logs and old bits of furniture while they were still dry, and storing them in some sheltered place, ready to be retrieved nearer the day itself in November. You needed a lot of stuff to build a huge bonfire, and it had to be collected over a period of time and be as dry as possible, so that it would blaze rather than just make smoke.

As August drew to an end, your mind was forced to start thinking about school again. Your mum would drag you out shopping for a new school blazer and some lovely new 'fish-box' shoes for you to wear for the new autumn term. You had mixed emotions about going back to school. On the one hand you wanted to see all the mates that you hadn't seen during the school break, but on the other hand you were nervous about going back to an unfamiliar new classroom and possibly new teachers. You also didn't want the summer to end, or to even think about the approaching dark evenings of autumn. The real anxiety came when you were eleven years old, and the time had arrived for you to start at a new secondary or grammar school – really nerve-wracking!

DINKY TOY

No. 400
B.E.V. Electric Truck
Price 2/9 each

No. 674
Austin Cha
Army Veh
with Driv
Length 2½ in.

No. 480
ord 10 cwt. Van "Kod
Length 3½ in. 2/9

No. 492
Loud Speake
Length 3½ in.

No. 158
Riley Saloon
Length 3½ in. 2/2

No. 441
Tanker Cas
Length 4½ in.

No. 641
my 1-Ton Cargo Truck
with Driver
Length 3½ in. 3/9

No. 621
3-Ton Army Wagon with Driver
Length 4¾ in. 5/3

No. 153
Standard Vangua
Length 3½ in.

No. 161
ustin Somerset Saloon
Length 3½ 2/2

No. 452
Trojan Van, 15 cwt.
Length 2¾ in. 2/6

No. 232
Alfa Romeo Rac
Length 4

Nine

CHRISTMAS

Christmas is always the most special time of year for children, and so it was in the 1950s. The festive season was much less commercialised than it is now, but then there was no Internet or telephone selling, and modern terms like 'marketing' and 'direct sales' weren't even in common use. Goods were mostly sold in shops, and sometimes through newspaper adverts or by door-to-door salesmen. We all believed in Father Christmas, and of course we still do! At Christmastime, young children would be taken to see Father Christmas in his grotto at the nearest department store. You would be encouraged to sit on his knee and tell him what you wanted for Christmas – nothing too big of course! This strange tradition contradicted everything you were taught about being wary of strangers – taking you into a small, scary, cave-like place and urging you to sit on the knee of a strange man who is dressed from head-to-toe in a bizarre disguise. It's no wonder that lots of terrified young children kicked and screamed their way out of the place!

Having already endured the post-war austerity years of the late 1940s and early '50s, many people were still struggling to make ends meet in the mid to late 1950s. Even the better-off families spent their money sparingly, if only out of habit, and it was just the lucky few that could expect to receive big expensive presents on Christmas morning. In schools, children were taught to focus on the true meaning of Christmas, and were encouraged to make the most of the events surrounding the whole of the Christmas period rather than just the presents they might get on Christmas morning.

Remember those wads of assorted coloured paper strips that you made paper chains with at primary school? Everyone in the class was given a bundle of them and put to work to make their own section of the chain, rolling each strip into a circle and fastening the ends with glue to form additional links. Gradually the paper chain grew in length until the combined sections were deemed to be long enough to link together and decorate the classroom walls. You will also have made other Christmas decorations to hang from the ceiling and fill in empty spaces on the walls, probably using crêpe paper. And best of all, you will have made Christmas cards and Advent calendars that you sprinkled with colour glitter, which got everywhere, even in your hair and up your nose. It was all cheap and cheerful, but the whole preparation process for Christmas was so exciting, at school and at home.

It seemed an age since the autumn half-term holiday, which was back in October, and it was over a month since the excitement of Guy Fawkes Night. There wasn't much to break the monotony in between the summer holidays

Magazines kept the family informed as to what a home should look like at Christmas.

and Christmas, and what with the dark nights of autumn being so cold and damp you just longed for Christmas to arrive and cheer everyone up! Unlike today, the Christmas season didn't really begin until well into December. It would be early in December before you would see the first real signs of Christmas on the high street, with shops decorating their windows to look festive. At about the same time, your school would start to plan for its customary Nativity play, and they would begin to organise choir practice for the Christmas carol concert. Once the school's Christmas activities got under way then the whole atmosphere around school was very different from the rest of the year. Even if you weren't chosen to play the back half of a donkey in the Christmas Nativity play, you could still help to make the costumes and the scenery for it. And, so what if you were only going to be second reserve for playing the triangle in the school band on the big day, you could still enjoy the rehearsals! Being chosen to help make the traditional classroom crib for baby Jesus was a big honour, and there were many disappointed volunteers, but learning to sing all those Christmas carols really did lift everyone's spirits. It was your first experience of do-it-yourself, fabricating an old cardboard box into a credible animal stable using very little in the way of materials; paint for the walls, cotton wool to represent snow on the roof, and straw to cover the floor of the stable – not forgetting a big shiny star made out of cardboard and covered in silver glitter. Once the stable was finished, you had to position all of the handmade Nativity crib figures inside: baby Jesus in a small straw-filled manger, Mary and Joseph, the three kings bearing gifts of gold, frankincense and myrrh, and the donkey – with as many other animals as you could fit in. There were always some funny looking camels – or perhaps they were sheep! It didn't matter if you came from a religious background or not, everyone got into the theatrical mood of Christmastime. Schoolwork was much less tedious during those few weeks in December because you were so immersed in the excitement and celebration of Christmas, and lessons were just something that happened in between. Your main thoughts didn't revolve around what you would be getting for Christmas, or how big your presents would be. You were caught up in the whole occasion of the season, and it was the combination of events that made it all so enjoyable. Usually, in primary school, shortly before you broke up for the Christmas holidays, you had your school Christmas party. If it was a big school then you probably had a party just for your class, with loads of jelly and fairy cakes, Christmas music, and games like pass the parcel and musical chairs. Christmas really was worth waiting all year for!

Christmas Shopping

These were times when women were not yet fully emancipated; there had been a lull of more than twenty years in feminist activities, and women's equality issues didn't spark off again until the 1960s when the second-wave feminist activists rose from behind the parapet to re-ignite the arguments for women's cultural and political equality. Working women of the 1950s were not paid the same rates as men, and men were considered to be the breadwinners in the family while women were thought of as homemakers, and whether they held down a full-time job or not, women were expected to look after the home and care for the children. They just couldn't shrug off the 'housewife' tag. The age of 'modern man' had not yet arrived, and 1950s men just didn't do washing, ironing or shopping. As a result, the task of Christmas shopping was left mainly to the woman of the house – your mum.

At Christmastime, more so than usual, you were probably enlisted as a reluctant bag carrier, following in your mum's footsteps as she trudged around every market stall, shop and department store on the high street, shopping for all those Christmas essentials. There were no shopping malls, supermarkets or self-service shops to brighten the shopping experience. Instead, there were loads of individual specialist shops, and shopping seemed to take ages, what with your mum stopping for endless chats about the weather with each shopkeeper, and dread the thought of her meeting a friend en route – that could take up an hour! Constantly weaving in and out of shops and between market stalls, the bags gradually got heavier and heavier, and if it was raining, you just got wet!

At Christmas, the high street atmosphere was so different to today. You didn't see people walking around with silly red Santa Claus hats and brightly coloured Bermuda shorts like you do now. People were much more reserved back then, and even got dressed up in a posh frock or a shirt and tie to go high street shopping. The shop window displays were always very Christmassy, particularly in the department stores, where windows were dressed with all sorts of wonderful festive scenes. Many a lost child would be found gazing through a department store's window at a display of lifelike mannequins and wondrous objects that had been arranged into a Christmas setting; he or she would be completely captivated by a scene that was worlds apart from their own lifestyle. The air around the street markets was filled with the smell of fresh pine Christmas trees, and the market stalls were strung with hundreds of coloured festoon lights. There was always a man on the corner roasting chestnuts over red-hot coals in a brazier – another great smell of Christmas! The Salvation Army band played festive music and sang carols, generating goodwill and encouraging everyone to drop a few coppers into the hat for charity.

In your eyes as a young child, Christmas shopping didn't include buying toys or presents for you or your siblings because Santa brought your presents on Christmas morning. Presents were bought for family and other people, but they always seemed to be boring presents, like scarves or socks – nothing exciting like a Davy Crockett hat or a high-speed glowing yo-yo. Even with all those marvellous toys, games and novelties on display in shop windows everywhere, your mum's main focus was on food. By the late 1950s, still only one in four families in Britain had a fridge, which meant that most working-class families managed to live without a fridge throughout the '50s. Mums needed to do a lot of strategic planning when buying food, drink and other perishables, particularly when there was the added burden of rationing in the early '50s. Food wasn't pre-packed in plastic as it is today, and nothing was date-stamped with use-by dates. You had to buy things as fresh as possible to get maximum use out of them, but there was no way of telling how long something had been in the shop, let alone how long it had been in the food processing chain. Mums acquired the skill of detecting the freshness of things like meat, fruit and dairy products; but however fresh the food was, without the use of a fridge your mum had to shop every couple of days to keep the family fed and avoid food going off. Unlike today, you couldn't just pop out to the shop at any time of the day or evening, seven days a week. In the 1950s, many shops were shut on Saturday afternoons, even large stores like John Lewis in London's Oxford Street. And, apart from the corner newsagent's shop that opened for a few hours on a Sunday morning, there were no shops whatsoever open on Sundays. On top of that, every area had its half-day closing each week, usually on a Tuesday, Wednesday or Thursday. Some shops didn't open at all on Mondays; again, John Lewis branches used to be closed on a Monday to give staff, known as Partners, a proper weekend break.

You really needed to know your local shopping area's opening and closing times, and plan your shopping needs around them. This was even more difficult at holiday times like Easter and Christmas, when all shops were shut during the bank (public) holidays. If Christmas Day happened to fall on a Monday then the last day for buying food was Saturday, and it would have to last until the following Wednesday when the shops opened for business again. Even on the Wednesday, other than on-site family bakers, most shops wouldn't have any fresh food stocks because nobody had been working over the Christmas period to produce them. Therefore, mums tried to buy enough food to last through until a couple of days after Christmas. This led to large pre-Christmas queues outside shops selling bread, vegetables and meat. Most mums placed advance orders with the shopkeepers but they still had to queue to collect their order. It wasn't unusual to see enormous queues gathering outside baker's shops on the day before and the day after a holiday. Bread was a very important part of a child's diet, often the cheapest and quickest remedy for your hunger pangs, and families didn't like to run out of it. Tinned meat and other tinned foods were also bought as a back-up. Then there were all the Christmas trimmings, like nuts and dates, Christmas crackers and balloons, and perhaps a few replacement decorations for the ones that were broken last year. Your dad was roped in to get the Christmas tree and to make sure there was enough coal or logs for the fire, and while he was at it he probably bought a few bottles of something 'special' to add some Christmas cheer. Even people that didn't usually keep any alcohol in the house would make sure they had a bottle of Sherry and a bottle of Port to offer visitors a Yuletide drink.

Christmas at Home

The tradition of sending Christmas cards is still very strong today, but in the 1950s few homes had telephones installed and so the only way to pass on Christmas greetings to family and friends was by way of Christmas cards, postcards or letters. This was another task usually left to mum – not much has changed in that regard! The build-up to Christmas started much later in the home than at school. There may have been some early recognition of it approaching; perhaps your dad had a go at making a doll's house, or your mum might have started knitting a 'lovely' Christmas jumper for some lucky recipient. Mostly, there was little evidence of Christmas until very near the day itself, when the decorations went up in the living room and a space was made for the tree. You probably also cleared a spot on the sideboard where the crib could go, and helped mum and dad to blow up the balloons – an impossible task for young lungs with little puff.

As Christmas started to get nearer, your mum would have had a good tidy-up to make sure that everything was spick and span for the big day. Positioning and decorating the Christmas tree, and hanging sprigs of holly and mistletoe from the ceiling, these were the things that signalled the start of Christmas in the home. Some people still followed the old tradition of putting candles on their trees for decoration ... Well, there were a lot of burned-out houses around in the 1950s! However, in the main, the Christmas tree would be decorated with baubles, bells, ribbons, chocolate coins wrapped in gold foil, and balls of cotton wool to represent snow, with the customary angel or fairy doll perched at the very top of the tree. Christmas tree lights, or fairy lights as they were sometimes called, didn't become popular in the home until the late '50s, and then they were expensive and could be very dangerous. Your first ever set of fairy lights probably came from Woolworths – they sold everything.

A few days before Christmas, your dad splashed out threepence to buy his 'once a year copy' of the *Radio Times* to see what exciting Christmas treats were on the radio and television over the Christmas week. Mum spent a lot of time in the kitchen making the Christmas cake, Christmas (plum) pudding, mince pies and sausage rolls. And you wrote your letter to Father Christmas in Lapland, telling him what presents you would like and begging him not to forget you.

Christmas itself was really short-lived, and it was only on Christmas Eve that the Christmas celebrations at home really began; that was usually after your dad got home from work. People tended to work long hours and there was no such thing as finishing work early on Christmas Eve. The night before Christmas was, in many ways, more exciting than the day itself. There weren't many Christmassy programmes on the radio or television, apart from carol concerts, and you might be treated to an adaptation of Charles Dickens' *A Christmas Carol*. Mostly, everyone was busy, wrapping individual family presents or helping mum to sort out last minute jobs around the house. A number of people went to midnight mass at their local church on Christmas Eve, which for some was just for the novelty of it, and for others it was to satisfy a once-a-year twinge of conscience, but mostly it was regular churchgoers that went every year.

Every child went through the ritual of leaving something in the fireplace for Santa when he came down the chimney to deliver the presents, but once again your dad managed to skate around the perpetual question, 'How will Santa get down the chimney without getting burned?' You decide to give up on that subject; maybe your dad isn't that clever after all! Instead, you pester your mum to see if it is time yet to put Santa's glass of milk and mince pie in the fireplace. Dad suggests that you leave a carrot out for Santa's reindeer, Rudolf, and that Santa would probably prefer a glass of Sherry instead of milk, but mum says that's not a good idea because after a glass of Sherry he could fall off the roof!

Suddenly, you are aware of the sound of carol singers in the street outside, and you rush to the window to see. There is a large group of people in the middle of the road holding song sheets and lanterns, and there are others going door-to-door collecting money. These are the last carol singers that you will see this Christmas and so you stay at the window to watch and listen, and your dad goes outside to

A shy young girl visits Father Christmas at Santa's Grotto in Gamages department store in central London in 1955.

give them some money. With the carol singers gone, it won't be long before you are tucked up in bed and dreaming the night away, hoping that Santa hasn't forgotten to bring your presents. Having searched the house one more time, you are still unable to find any presents that your mum and dad might have hidden away from you, and so you go off to bed early in the hope that morning will come quicker. Before climbing into bed, you reposition the empty stocking (optimists used a pillow case) that is hanging at the end of your bed, just to be sure that Santa will find it easily and without having to search for it. Once in bed, you close your eyes and try to stay awake as long as possible, in the hope that you might see Santa when he comes to your house, but as the minutes tick away, you gradually slip into a dreamy slumber.

Soon it is morning, and even though it's very early, not even the cold air in the bedroom can deter you from climbing out from under the blankets to investigate the bulging stocking at the end of your bed. Nothing too exciting in there, but you are very happy to find it filled with the usual Christmas mix of sweets and other goodies. You know that your parents are still sleeping, but you deliberately make noises to wake them up in the hope that the day can begin. After all, it is Christmas!

Family life was much more organised back then; people tended to get up at a routine time each day, even on weekends and holidays. Meals were usually at fixed times, and you were expected to be at the table on time. Although there wasn't much difference in the way most families organised their Christmas Day, with breakfast, church, dinner, Queen's speech, and sandwiches and cake for tea; there was some inconsistency when it came down to opening presents. In some families, everyone just dived in once the whole household was up, with wrapping paper flying everywhere. Not a bad plan, because it gave children the whole day in which to play with their new toys and games, keeping them occupied, and hopefully quiet. Other families went to church on Christmas morning and the presents were left until after they got home. Different families had different rules for when presents could be opened, like after breakfast, or after Christmas dinner when all the family was together, or maybe when granny arrived. These were all very polite ways of doing things, but a bit mean on the kids!

There were always one or two children out in the street early on Christmas morning trying out their new roller skates or hula hoop, more so in the late '50s when people were a bit flusher with money. It was pitiful to watch this from the window, while your own presents were still neatly wrapped up under the Christmas tree. Some kids weren't even allowed out of the house at all on Christmas Day, which was hard to take if you got a new scooter for Christmas … real torture! Christmas presents improved as you moved through the '50s and further away from the frugal post-war years. If you were lucky, you would get at least one big present, a wind-up toy, a big doll, an Airfix model or Meccano construction kit, or a board game or something. Almost everything else would be what adults would call 'practical', like socks or a set of cotton handkerchiefs with your initial embroidered in one corner of each hankie. Faraway relatives would sometimes send you money, and those were the best presents of all.

Everyone got dressed in their Sunday best on Christmas Day, even if they were staying at home. Typical 1950s dads didn't do casual anyway, collar and tie was always the order of the day. The table was laid early for Christmas dinner, with all the best glasses and cutlery, and of course the Christmas crackers. The dinner always seemed to be served sharp at one o'clock, and it was somehow important to be finished in time for the Queen's speech. Many families had roast chicken for Christmas dinner instead of the traditional turkey, as turkey was too expensive. Goose was also popular, but again, it was dearer than chicken. Your plate was filled to the brim with roast potatoes, stuffing, and all sorts of fresh vegetables. When you were stuffed full of Christmas dinner, your mum would bring in the Christmas pudding, into which she had already put some threepenny and sixpenny pieces. It was considered to be lucky if you found one in your piece of pudding – extra lucky if you broke a tooth on one! As was the tradition, your dad would pour some of his Christmas brandy over the pudding and set fire to it. You would then struggle to eat the smallest piece of what was a very rich plum pudding, whilst trying to avoid swallowing one of the coins that were buried somewhere inside it.

In between dinner and teatime you would munch on a variety of snacks laid out on the sideboard, from chestnuts to marshmallows. It was the only day in the year that you could really stuff yourself silly. At some point during the afternoon, you would be prised away from your favourite toy to go for a walk out in the fresh air, to 'help your dinner go down'. On Christmas Day in 1956, you wouldn't have needed much encouragement to go outside, because it was one of those rare Christmas days when snow fell in most areas of the country and answered every child's Christmas wish for a white Christmas. There wasn't much to watch on television during the day, and most families only switched it on for the Queen's speech at three o'clock (from 1957). There was often a live broadcast from a children's ward at one of the hospitals, and *Billy Smart's Circus* was usually on in the afternoon.

Later in the afternoon, just as you finished chewing on a date, your mum would start to serve afternoon tea. Cold turkey and ham sandwiches, sausage rolls and pickled onions, with lots of sweet things, like mince pies, Victoria sponge cake, fruit jelly and blancmange. After tea, mum would hand around her box of Black Magic chocolates that your dad had bought her, while dad would puff away on one of the half corona cigars that he had received. Apart from game shows, and perhaps a special drama production, the evening's television highlight was the big variety show that the BBC put on every year, with all the best acts of the day. In the early '50s it was the BBC's *Television's Christmas Party*, a live variety show that was on for about an hour and a half, and featured artists like Arthur Askey, Max Bygraves, Tommy Cooper, Frankie Howerd, Bob Monkhouse, Terry Thomas and Norman Wisdom. In the late '50s there was BBC's *Christmas Night with the Stars*, a grander pre-recorded variety and sketch show, featuring artists like Charlie Chester, Billy Cotton, Charlie Drake, Jimmy Edwards, Tony Hancock, Ted Ray and Jack Warner.

Sometimes, families would play board games in the evening, and when there was a family gathering with aunts and uncles and grandparents, the grown-ups would have a singsong around the old upright piano, or play gramophone records and talk. They were all so old! And it was all so boring! Later in the evening, when the novelty of playing with your new toys and games had worn off, you would all play cards together as a family, and you may even have convinced them to let you listen to one of your favourite gramophone records.

All of the day's excitement and your continual gorging eventually took its toll on you, and you had to admit to being tired enough for bed. Tripping over the pile of gramophone records on the floor next to the record player, you sleepily make your way off to bed, while the grown-ups continue to play cards into the early hours of the morning.

The next day, Boxing Day, was still considered to be a family day when you stayed indoors, had visitors, or went to visit relatives. If you were lucky, you would get a couple of hours to play outside with your friends and try out some of their Christmas presents. Boxing Day was very much like a Sunday; all the shops were shut and there was nothing to do. The only available treat was a trip to the circus, if you had one within travelling distance of where you lived and your parents could afford it. Grown-ups had to go back to work on 27 December so Boxing Day was their last day off for a while (New Year's Day wasn't a national public holiday in the '50s). Boxing day, therefore, was usually a stay-at-home family day.

In Scotland, Christmas was not celebrated to the same extent as it was in the rest of Britain, and up until 1958 Christmas Day was a normal working day. For almost 400 years Christmas was banned in Scotland, where it was seen as a Popish or Catholic festival. Scotland's main day of celebration was Hogmanay (31 December) and it was celebrated with public holidays from 31 December – 2 January.

Ten

MEMORABLE 1950S EVENTS

Sitting cross-legged on the floor, you move your knees up and curl your arms around them to make more room for the other kids sitting on the floor around you. You are aware that the room is full, but you are oblivious to who is actually sitting beside you because your concentration is fixed on the huge wooden cabinet in the corner of the room, just an arm's length away from you. Your attention is broken for a moment when a grown-up leans over you and turns one of the knobs on the front of the cabinet – click! The room becomes hushed and you are now aware of a slight humming noise coming from the stretched brown and gold cloth that is set into the bottom half of the cabinet's fascia. One of the boys starts to get impatient for something to happen, and a grown-up voice from behind tells him to be quiet, 'Wait a minute, it needs to warm up.' Soon, a picture starts to appear in the grey twelve-inch glass screen, which is set into the top half of the cabinet. Everyone stares at the silvery-grey moving images that are now clearly visible on the screen, and the excitement in the room begins to mount.

The Queen's Coronation

On Tuesday 2 June 1953, an estimated 3 million people lined the streets of London to see the procession of their newly crowned queen, Elizabeth II. Most of them spent the night before dossing down on pavements to secure a good vantage point for the morning. By eleven o'clock on that Tuesday morning, the majority of the country's remaining population had settled down to listen to the commentary on the radio, or to watch the live broadcast on BBC television, or at public venue screenings in cinemas, church halls and hospitals. Most of the television viewers had gathered in groups at neighbours' houses to watch their queen crowned. All over the country there were rows of empty houses, where whole families had decanted into their neighbours' crowded living rooms to watch the ceremony on tiny silvery-grey television screens; most screens measured only twelve or fourteen inches, but some were as small as nine inches.

It rained on the day, but that certainly didn't dampen the celebrations. Memories of Queen Elizabeth's coronation are etched into the minds of every 1950s child. It was the first time ever that a monarch's coronation had been televised for all to see. It brightened up the lives of ordinary people who were still suffering economic hardship and scarcity in post-war Britain. The queen's gold ornate coronation coach, and the extravagant ceremony with all

In 1953, in a street in central London, a group of young children pose for a picture to be taken just before their 'Queen's Coronation' street party begins.

Children and adults gathered together for a 'Queen's Coronation' street party in south-east London in 1953.

the dignitaries in their fine robes and jewels, gave ordinary people a peek into the land of plenty.

After seeing the wondrous real-life fairy story of royalty on television, the biggest celebrations began, with street parties in every town and village across the land. People brought out tables from their houses and placed them side-by-side to form one long table down the centre of the road. Everyone was enlisted to carry chairs from houses and line them up along each side of the extended table. The table was then dressed from end to end with lots of clean white tablecloths. Street lampposts were decorated, flags hung from upstairs windows and whole streets were decked out in red, white and blue bunting and cardboard cut-out royal crowns. There were all sorts of special coronation items for people to use and wear, like cardboard hats, paper aprons, bibs and napkins. There were loads of sandwiches, cakes and jelly, and everyone was happy and friendly. Most kids wore their best clothes or their school uniform, but some streets had fancy dress parties and the children wore a variety of outfits and strange homemade hats. The queen's coronation was probably the most memorable 1950s childhood event, apart from the day sweet rationing ended! Oh, and the day you got your first ever television set.

The Festival of Britain

Thursday 3 May 1951 was the official opening day of the festival at the main exhibition venue, which was at London's South Bank site by the River Thames, near to Waterloo Bridge. The Festival of Britain was spread over a four-month period and included a series of exhibitions held all around the country. It was organised in an attempt to provide the British people with a feeling that the country was recovering from all the destruction caused to its towns and cities during the Second World War. The exhibitions were intended to lift people's spirits whilst promoting the very best of British design, science, art and industry. London's South Bank site, including The Royal Festival Hall, was especially constructed to be the centrepiece of the festival. Other South Bank structures included the Dome of Discovery, a temporary building that was like an early version of the Millennium Dome, and the Skylon, an unusual cigar-shaped aluminium-clad steel tower supported

Visitors to the Festival of Britain outside the Dome of Discovery on London's South Bank in 1951.

by cables – all designed in a modernist style. The festival also celebrated the centenary of the Great Exhibition of 1851, sometimes referred to as the Crystal Palace Exhibition.

Festival of Britain exhibitions were held in all of the main cities around Britain, but the most popular visitor sites were in London, with 8.5 million people visiting the South Bank Exhibition, and 8 million visiting the Festival Pleasure Gardens in Battersea. Most children would have enjoyed something about the festival, even if they were unable to visit any of the exhibition sites, because there were organised street parties all over the country, with bunting and Union Jacks everywhere.

End of Rationing 1953/4

Food, clothing and petrol rationing was introduced at the start of the Second World War, but rationing got even stricter after the war ended, with bread and potatoes being added to the long list of foodstuffs in short supply. Children born in the 1930s and 1940s thought that it was normal to live with rationed amounts of food. The rationing rules were gradually relaxed from the end of the '40s, but the biggest cause of celebration was when sweet rationing ended in February 1953, closely followed by the end of sugar rationing in September of that same year. Britain saw the final end of all rationing at midnight on 4 July 1954, when restrictions on the sale and purchase of meat and bacon were lifted. It was, by then, nine years since the war had ended, and fourteen years since food rationing had first begun.

The Age of Television

It was the decade that television really started to overtake radio as the most popular form of entertainment in the home. Even as late as 1949, two out of three people in Britain had never seen a television programme. Television ownership really took off early in 1953, with people queuing to get one installed to watch the queen's coronation. There was a further boost when Independent Television first started broadcasting commercially funded television programmes in September 1955. By 1957, radio audience figures had dropped significantly, with the BBC acknowledging that the nightly audience figures had fallen by one million in the last year alone, with more and more people moving to television viewing. By 1959, the number of British households with a television set had increased to 10 million. The numbers had been increasing at a rate of about one million each year for the previous six years. The 1950s was the age of television and it completely changed our way of life. It brought a wealth of new entertainment to everyone, but mostly to a generation of kids that had previously been starved of so many of life's luxuries. There were loads of brand new children's programmes, including some much-cherished and fondly remembered ones like *Crackerjack* (1955) and *Blue Peter* (1958).

Rock and Roll

The '50s saw the arrival of 'rock and roll' music in Britain for the first time (1954–6). This new wave of popular culture was introduced to us through teenage films and records from the USA, with American rock and roll artists like Bill Haley and his Comets, and Elvis Presley the 'King of Rock and Roll'. Britain had never known anything like it. It stirred British teenagers into life and had them jiving in the aisles at their local cinemas. Soon, ordinary British teenagers began to follow suit, buying guitars and forming their own skiffle and rock groups. It was the start of music careers for celebrated British artists like Lonnie Donegan, Adam Faith, Billy Fury, Cliff Richard and Marty Wilde. The rest is history!

All gramophone records were made in large size 78s (78 rpm) format until 1949 when RCA Victor developed the 7-inch 45-rpm single. However, few people owned a record player suitable for playing the new 45s, and so the older 78s continued to be sold alongside the 45s well into the 1950s. In 1958, Audio Fidelity in the USA, and Pye in Britain, issued the first stereo two-channel records, but we had to wait until the 1960s to see them sold in any quantity in Britain because very few people had stereo record players in the 1950s.

Eleven

WHATEVER HAPPENED TO?

Billy Fury. After achieving a handful of hit singles in 1959, Billy went on to have another twenty-three hit singles in the 1960s, but he suffered from heart problems and was forced to become much less active. Despite ongoing trouble with his heart, he continued to work through until his death in 1983. Sadly, on 27 January 1983, he collapsed after returning home from the recording studio, and died the next morning at the age of forty-two.

Bobbies on the Beat. In the 1950s, we were all used to seeing Bobbies walking the beat, but there are far fewer sightings of them nowadays. In the 1960s, in some suburban and rural areas, some were put into police 'Panda cars' to replace beat Bobbies, while in other areas the Panda cars worked alongside beat Bobbies. In the 1980s, it became common practice for the police to patrol in pairs, which again reduced the sightings of 'Bobbies on the beat' by half, and this figure was trimmed even further by the increased amount of time they had to spend doing paperwork at the police station. But, there is hope for Londoners! In March 2009, the Metropolitan Police Commissioner, Sir Paul Stephenson, announced that he would be getting police officers to walk the beat on their own rather than in pairs, to double the number of patrols.

Bus Conductors. The old-style double-decker buses that we were all familiar with required two-person crews to operate them, because the layout of the vehicle separated the driver from the passenger areas. Therefore, a conductor was needed to collect fares and to see passengers on and off the bus. Since the early 1970s, there has been a steady increase in newly designed 'one-person operation' buses that allow the driver access to the passenger area, and the ability to perform the tasks previously done by conductors. Conductor operation finally ceased in London in 2005.

Corporal Punishment in Schools. In 1986, physical punishment was abolished in all the UK's state-run schools, and in 1998 it was outlawed in all independent schools.

Dave King. In the 1960s, this popular '50s entertainer went to the USA for a short period, after which he returned to England where he found that his style of comedy had fallen out of favour. He later became a television character actor. He died in 2002 following a short illness, at the age of seventy-three.

Diana Dors. She continued to star in films and appear in television dramas, comedies and game shows until shortly before her death in 1984. She died of cancer on 4 May aged fifty-two. Although she left clues to its whereabouts, the mystery of her missing £2 million fortune has never been solved. She is believed to have hidden it away in various bank accounts across Europe before she was taken ill.

A policeman on point duty directing traffic in London's Ludgate Hill in the
early 1950s.

Dickie Valentine. This very popular 1950s singer's fame diminished in the 1960s, but he continued to perform until he died in a car accident in 1971, at the age of forty-one.

Free School Milk. Abolished for seven- to eleven-year-olds in 1971 by Margaret Thatcher when she became Secretary of State for Education and Science, as part of Prime Minister Edward Heath's spending cuts.

Gert and Daisy. The popular female comedy duo, and sisters, Elsie and Doris Waters, created these two cockney characters. Elsie and Doris wrote all their own material, and their quick-fire comedy conversations of one-liners and comic songs kept everyone entertained throughout the 1930s, '40s and '50s, on both radio and gramophone record. In the 1960s, their popularity diminished, and they went into semi-retirement at their home in Sussex. They continued to do the occasional nostalgia shows until Doris fell ill in the 1970s. Doris died in 1978 (aged seventy-four), and Elsie died in 1990 (aged ninety-five).

Jimmy Clitheroe. He entertained us for forty years in every medium of show business, but is best known for his long-running radio show *The Clitheroe Kid*, which featured the diminutive Jimmy playing the part of a cheeky schoolboy. In his personal life he was a very private man, who lived a quiet life with his mother in a semi-detached bungalow in Blackpool. In June 1973, he sadly died from an accidental overdose of sleeping pills, on the same day as his mother's funeral. He was fifty-one.

London Pea-soupers (Smog). Anyone that lived in London during the 1950s will remember the dense fogs that would descend in the form of yellowish smog, caused by cold fog mixing with coal fire emissions. They were called 'pea-soupers' because they had the consistency of thick pea soup, and many people died from the effects of breathing the smog. In 1956, the British government introduced the Clean Air Act and created smokeless zones in the capital. This reduced the sulphur dioxide levels to such a degree that London's intense yellow smogs became a thing of the past.

Marty Wilde. The popularity of his singing style diminished in the 1960s with the arrival of new styles of music from the USA and the advent of the home-grown Merseybeat sound. Marty went on to influence and help his daughter Kim Wilde become a major international pop star in the 1980s. He has continued to write music and has established himself as a premier act on rock and roll nostalgia concert tours, which he still continues to do at the age of seventy.

Mr Pastry (Richard Hearne). He entertained us on BBC TV and on film for thirty years, and he was equally popular in the USA with frequent appearances on the *Ed Sullivan Show*. His slapstick Mr Pastry comedy went out of favour in the 1960s, but he continued to do lots of charity work around London and near to his home in Kent. He was made president of the Lords Taverners charity in 1963, and was awarded the OBE in 1970 for his services to charity. It is rumoured that he was offered the role of Doctor Who when Jon Pertwee left the series in 1973, but Hearne wanted to play the part in the character of Mr Pastry, and the offer was withdrawn. He died in 1979 at the age of seventy-one.

Mrs Dale's Diary **(Radio Serial Drama)**. The comforting tales from Mrs Dale's diary that were played out daily on the BBC Light Programme since 1948 were considered to be too old fashioned for 1960s listeners, and in 1962 the format was changed and the series was renamed *The Dales*. This helped to postpone its demise, but after having transferred to the newly created BBC Radio 2 in 1967, Mrs Dale was finally taken off-air in 1969.

National Service (Peacetime Conscription). In the 1950s, the thought of doing 'National Service' was on the mind of every young boy as they entered their teenage years. At the time, every healthy man between eighteen and twenty-one was expected to serve in the armed forces for two years, and remain on the reserve list for three and a half years. Call-up papers would arrive on or after one's eighteenth birthday, but the obligation would cease after the age of twenty-six. National Service formally ended on 31 December 1960, but those who had deferred service, for reasons such as University studies or on compassionate grounds, still had to complete their National Service after this date.

Police Boxes. The old police boxes, once a familiar sight on city streets, with a few exceptions, were phased out from about 1969 in favour of modern portable tele-communications. Back in 1953, there were 685 of the easily recognisable blue police boxes on the streets of London.

Police Whistles. They were phased out during the late '60s and early '70s, when it was considered that the increase in traffic noise made them inaudible in urban areas. They were replaced by the early hand-held police radios.

Ruby Murray. Her successful 1950s hit record and film career ended at the start of the 1960s, but she continued to appear in cabaret and nostalgia shows around Britain until

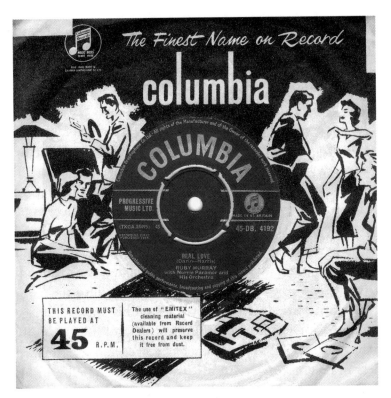

Real Love was just one of many top twenty hit records that Ruby Murray had in the 1950s. It reached number 18 in the UK charts in December 1958.

shortly before her death in 1996. A compilation CD album of her hits was released in 1989, and an anthology triple CD album in 2005. Her name is still used in cockney rhyming slang to describe a curry, as in 'a Ruby' or 'a Ruby Murray'. She died of liver cancer in December 1996 aged sixty-one in Torquay.

Smith's Crisps (with the little twist bag of salt). Now indirectly owned by the New York-based company, PepsiCo. Since the 1990s, the Smith's crisps brands have gradually been changed over to the Walker's crisps brand, but there are still some out there.

Telegram Messenger Boys. These young boys in their navy blue uniforms and pillbox caps were familiar sights on our streets in the 1950s. The urgent messages they carried usually contained bad news, but they were a valuable service at the time. In the 1930s, 65 million telegrams were being delivered each year and the service employed 11,000 staff. In 1965, the number of telegrams delivered was down to 10 million. By 1976, most telegrams were being delivered by post, telephone or telex, rather than by hand. The continuing improvements in telecommunications eventually led to their demise, and in 1977 the Post Office decided to abolish the telegram service, although it lingered on until 1981.

Tommy Steele. In the 1960s he left his pop idol image behind and became successful in stage and film musicals, which he continued with for many years. He has performed less in recent years, with his last appearance being in his revival of *Scrooge, the Musical* at the London Palladium in 2005, when he was sixty-nine.

Tony Hancock. He continued to star in his own comedy TV series and appear in films well into the 1960s, but he suffered from alcoholism and depression for a long time. In 1968, he committed suicide by an overdose in a Sydney hotel room aged forty-three. At the time, he had completed only three programmes of a thirteen-part series that he was doing for Australian television called *Hancock Down Under*.

Trolleybuses. These gradually ceased operation during the 1960s in favour of motorised buses. London saw the end of trolleybuses in 1962, and the last UK trolleybus service to stop operating was in Bradford in 1972.